55 Greek Recipes for Home

By: Kelly Johnson

Table of Contents

Appetizers:
- Tzatziki (Yogurt and Cucumber Dip)
- Spanakopita (Spinach and Feta Pie)
- Dolma (Stuffed Grape Leaves)
- Melitzanosalata (Eggplant Dip)
- Taramasalata (Fish Roe Dip)
- Keftedes (Greek Meatballs)
- Fasolada (Greek Bean Soup)
- Hummus Greek-style with Kalamata Olives
- Saganaki (Fried Cheese)
- Greek Salad Skewers

Main Courses:
- Moussaka (Eggplant and Meat Casserole)
- Souvlaki (Grilled Meat Skewers)
- Yiouvetsi (Baked Orzo with Meat)
- Gemista (Stuffed Vegetables)
- Kotopoulo Lemonato (Greek Lemon Chicken)
- Psari Plaki (Baked Fish)
- Keftethes me Saltsa Domata (Meatballs in Tomato Sauce)
- Arni Lemonato (Lamb in Lemon Sauce
- Garides Saganaki (Shrimp in Tomato and Feta Sauce)

Side Dishes:
- Gigantes Plaki (Baked Giant Beans)
- Horta Vrasta (Boiled Greens)
- Spanakorizo (Spinach and Rice)
- Fasolakia (Greek Green Beans)
- Revithia (Chickpea Soup)
- Kolokithokeftedes (Zucchini Fritters)
- Riganada (Greek Bread Salad)
- Briam (Greek Ratatouille)
- Manestra (greek Orzo Pasta)
- Patates Lemonates (Lemon Potatoes)

Desserts:
- Baklava (Phyllo and Nut Pastry
- Galaktoboureko (Custard Pastry)
- Loukoumades (Honey Puffs)
- Koulourakia (Butter Cookies)
- Karidopita (Walnut Cake)
- Ravani (Semolina Cake)

- Revani me Fasolakia (Semolina Cake with Green Beans)
- Diples (Fried Pastry)
- Karydopita me Pagoto (Walnut Cake with Ice Cream)
- Sokolatopita (Chocolate Cake)

Breads and Pastries:

- Fougasse (Greek Bread)
- Tiropita (Cheese Pie)
- Bougatsa (Custard-Filled Pastry)
- Koulouri Thessalonikis (Sesame Seed Bread Rings)
- Lagana (Clean Monday Flatbread)

Beverages:

- Greek Frappe Coffee
- Greek Mountain Tea (Tsai Tou Vounou)
- Tiropita (Cheese Pie)
- Ouzo Cocktail
- Mastiha Liqueur
- Retsina Wine

Breakfast Items:

- Bougatsa me Krema (Custard-Filled Pastry)
- Strapatsada (Tomato and Scrambled Eggs)
- Koulouri Thessalonikis (Sesame Seed Bread Rings)
- Greek Yogurt with Honey and Nuts
- Tyropita (Cheese Pie)

Tzatziki (Yogurt and Cucumber Dip) Recipe

Ingredients:

- 1 cucumber, finely grated
- 1 1/2 cups Greek yogurt
- 2 cloves garlic, minced
- 1 tablespoon extra-virgin olive oil
- 1 tablespoon fresh lemon juice
- 1 tablespoon fresh dill, chopped
- Salt and pepper to taste

Instructions:

1. Prepare the Cucumber:

   - Peel and finely grate the cucumber. Place the grated cucumber in a clean kitchen towel and squeeze out excess moisture.

2. Combine Yogurt and Cucumber:

   - In a mixing bowl, combine the Greek yogurt and grated cucumber.

3. Add Garlic:

   - Add the minced garlic to the yogurt and cucumber mixture. Adjust the amount of garlic to your taste preference.

4. Season with Olive Oil and Lemon Juice:

   - Drizzle extra-virgin olive oil and fresh lemon juice over the yogurt mixture.

5. Add Fresh Dill:

   - Stir in the chopped fresh dill. Dill adds a distinctive flavor to the tzatziki.

6. Season with Salt and Pepper:

   - Season the tzatziki with salt and pepper to taste. Mix well to combine all the ingredients.

7. Chill:

- Cover the tzatziki and refrigerate for at least 1-2 hours before serving. Chilling allows the flavors to meld.

8. Serve:

- Serve the tzatziki chilled, either as a dip or a sauce.

9. Optional Garnish:

- Optionally, garnish with a drizzle of olive oil and a sprig of fresh dill before serving.

10. Enjoy:

- Enjoy this refreshing and tangy Tzatziki as a dip for pita bread, vegetables, or as a sauce for grilled meats.

Tzatziki is a versatile and flavorful condiment that complements a variety of dishes. Whether served as a dip or a sauce, it adds a refreshing and herby element to your meals.

Spanakopita (Spinach and Feta Pie) Recipe

Ingredients:

For the Filling:

- 1 pound (about 450g) fresh spinach, washed and chopped
- 1 cup feta cheese, crumbled
- 1 cup ricotta cheese
- 1 cup Greek yogurt
- 1 cup green onions, finely chopped
- 3 eggs, lightly beaten
- 1/4 cup fresh dill, chopped
- Salt and pepper to taste
- Olive oil for brushing

For the Pastry:

- 1 package (about 16 ounces) phyllo dough, thawed
- 1 cup unsalted butter, melted

Instructions:

1. Prepare the Filling:

   - In a large skillet, wilt the chopped spinach over medium heat. Allow it to cool and squeeze out excess moisture.

2. Combine Filling Ingredients:

   - In a large mixing bowl, combine the wilted spinach, crumbled feta cheese, ricotta cheese, Greek yogurt, chopped green onions, beaten eggs, chopped dill, salt, and pepper. Mix well until all ingredients are evenly incorporated.

3. Preheat Oven:

   - Preheat your oven to 375°F (190°C).

4. Prepare Phyllo Dough:

- Unroll the thawed phyllo dough and cover it with a damp cloth to prevent it from drying out. Brush one sheet of phyllo dough with melted butter and place another sheet on top. Repeat until you have about 8-10 layers.

5. Add Filling and Fold:

- Spoon a portion of the spinach and feta filling along one edge of the phyllo layers. Roll the phyllo dough over the filling to create a log or cylinder shape. Place the rolled spanakopita on a baking sheet.

6. Repeat and Arrange:

- Repeat the process to make additional spanakopita rolls. Arrange them on the baking sheet with the seam side down.

7. Brush with Butter:

- Brush the tops of the spanakopita rolls with melted butter.

8. Bake:

- Bake in the preheated oven for 30-35 minutes or until the phyllo dough is golden brown and crispy.

9. Cool and Slice:

- Allow the spanakopita to cool for a few minutes before slicing into individual portions.

10. Serve:

- Serve the spanakopita warm as an appetizer, side dish, or light meal.

11. Enjoy:

- Enjoy the delicious layers of flaky phyllo dough and the savory spinach and feta filling in this classic Greek dish!

Spanakopita is a flavorful and satisfying dish that showcases the delicious combination of spinach and feta wrapped in crispy phyllo dough. It's a perfect addition to any Mediterranean-inspired meal.

Dolma (Stuffed Grape Leaves) Recipe

Ingredients:

For the Filling:

- 1 cup long-grain rice
- 1 cup water
- 1/2 cup pine nuts, toasted
- 1/2 cup currants or raisins
- 1 medium-sized onion, finely chopped
- 2 tablespoons olive oil
- 1/4 cup fresh parsley, finely chopped
- 1/4 cup fresh mint, finely chopped
- Salt and pepper to taste

For the Grape Leaves:

- 1 jar of grape leaves in brine, rinsed and drained
- Water for boiling grape leaves
- Lemon slices for garnish (optional)

Instructions:

1. Prepare the Grape Leaves:

- Rinse the grape leaves under cold water and separate them carefully to avoid tearing. If using jarred grape leaves, soak them in warm water for 15-20 minutes to reduce their briny taste. Rinse and drain.

2. Prepare the Filling:

- In a saucepan, combine the rice and water. Bring to a boil, then reduce heat to low, cover, and simmer until the rice is cooked and water is absorbed (about 15-20 minutes).

3. Toast Pine Nuts:

- In a dry skillet, toast the pine nuts over medium heat until they are lightly browned. Be careful not to burn them. Set aside.

4. Sauté Onion:

   - In a separate pan, sauté the finely chopped onion in olive oil until it becomes translucent.

5. Mix Filling Ingredients:

   - In a large bowl, combine the cooked rice, toasted pine nuts, sautéed onion, currants or raisins, chopped parsley, chopped mint, salt, and pepper. Mix the filling ingredients thoroughly.

6. Assemble Dolma:

   - Place a grape leaf on a flat surface, shiny side down, and add a spoonful of the rice mixture near the stem end. Fold the sides of the leaf over the filling and roll tightly to form a compact cylinder. Repeat with the remaining grape leaves and filling.

7. Arrange in Pot:

   - In a large pot, arrange the stuffed grape leaves tightly in layers, seam side down. You can add lemon slices between the layers for added flavor if desired.

8. Cook Dolma:

   - Pour enough water over the dolma to cover them. Place a heatproof plate on top to keep them in place during cooking. Cover the pot and simmer over low heat for about 45-60 minutes or until the grape leaves are tender.

9. Cool and Serve:

   - Allow the dolma to cool before serving. You can serve them warm or at room temperature.

10. Garnish (Optional):

    - Garnish the dolma with lemon slices before serving if desired.

11. Enjoy:

- Enjoy these flavorful and aromatic stuffed grape leaves as a delicious appetizer or part of a Mediterranean feast!

Melitzanosalata (Eggplant Dip) Recipe

Ingredients:

- 2 large eggplants
- 2 cloves garlic, minced
- 1/4 cup extra-virgin olive oil
- 2 tablespoons fresh lemon juice
- 2 tablespoons Greek yogurt (optional)
- Salt and pepper to taste
- Fresh parsley, chopped (for garnish)
- Olives and cherry tomatoes (for serving, optional)
- Pita bread or pita chips (for serving)

Instructions:

1. Roast or Grill Eggplants:

   - Preheat your oven to 400°F (200°C) or heat a grill. Prick the eggplants with a fork and roast them in the oven for about 45-60 minutes or on the grill until the skin is charred and the flesh is soft. Turn them occasionally for even cooking.

2. Peel Eggplants:

   - Allow the roasted or grilled eggplants to cool. Peel off the skin, leaving only the soft flesh.

3. Mash Eggplant Flesh:

   - In a bowl, mash the eggplant flesh with a fork or use a food processor for a smoother consistency.

4. Add Garlic:

   - Add minced garlic to the mashed eggplant.

5. Incorporate Olive Oil and Lemon Juice:

   - Drizzle extra-virgin olive oil and fresh lemon juice over the eggplant mixture. Mix well to combine.

6. Add Greek Yogurt (Optional):

    - If desired, add Greek yogurt to the mixture for a creamier texture. Mix until well incorporated.

7. Season with Salt and Pepper:

    - Season the melitzanosalata with salt and pepper to taste. Adjust the seasoning according to your preference.

8. Chill (Optional):

    - Refrigerate the dip for at least 1-2 hours to allow the flavors to meld. This step is optional but enhances the taste.

9. Garnish:

    - Before serving, garnish the melitzanosalata with fresh chopped parsley.

10. Serve:

    - Serve the eggplant dip with pita bread, pita chips, or as a side dish. Optionally, garnish with olives and cherry tomatoes.

11. Enjoy:

    - Enjoy the rich, smoky flavor of melitzanosalata as a delightful appetizer or accompaniment to your Mediterranean meals!

Melitzanosalata is a traditional Greek eggplant dip that offers a delicious blend of smoky roasted or grilled eggplant with the freshness of garlic, olive oil, and lemon. It's a versatile and flavorful dish that's perfect for spreading on bread or enjoying with your favorite dippables.

Taramasalata (Fish Roe Dip) Recipe

Ingredients:

- 200g (about 7 ounces) tarama (fish roe)
- 2 slices of white bread, crusts removed
- 1 small onion, grated
- 2 cloves garlic, minced
- 1/2 cup extra-virgin olive oil
- 2 tablespoons white wine vinegar or lemon juice
- 1 boiled potato, mashed (optional, for texture)
- Salt and pepper to taste
- Fresh parsley, chopped (for garnish)
- Olives and cucumber slices (for serving, optional)
- Pita bread or crackers (for serving)

Instructions:

1. Soak Bread:

- Soak the crustless white bread slices in water for a few minutes, then squeeze out excess water.

2. Blend Tarama:

- In a food processor, blend the tarama (fish roe) until smooth.

3. Add Soaked Bread:

- Add the soaked bread to the blended tarama and continue to blend until the mixture is well combined.

4. Incorporate Onion and Garlic:

- Add the grated onion and minced garlic to the tarama mixture. Blend until the onion and garlic are fully incorporated.

5. Gradually Add Olive Oil:

- With the food processor running, gradually add the extra-virgin olive oil in a steady stream until the mixture becomes a smooth paste.

6. Add Vinegar or Lemon Juice:

- Add white wine vinegar or lemon juice to the mixture and blend until well combined.

7. Incorporate Mashed Potato (Optional):

- If using, add the mashed boiled potato to the mixture for a creamier texture. Blend until smooth.

8. Season:

- Season the taramasalata with salt and pepper to taste. Adjust the seasoning according to your preference.

9. Chill (Optional):

- Refrigerate the taramasalata for at least 1-2 hours to allow the flavors to develop. This step is optional but enhances the taste.

10. Garnish:

- Before serving, garnish the taramasalata with chopped fresh parsley.

11. Serve:

- Serve the fish roe dip with pita bread, crackers, or as a spread. Optionally, garnish with olives and cucumber slices.

12. Enjoy:

- Enjoy the unique flavor of taramasalata as a delightful appetizer or dip for your Mediterranean-inspired meals!

Taramasalata is a classic Greek dip made with fish roe, creating a rich and savory spread with a unique taste. It's a perfect addition to your meze platter or as a dip for various breads and crackers.

Keftedes (Greek Meatballs) Recipe

Ingredients:

For the Meatballs:

- 1 pound ground beef or a mixture of beef and lamb
- 1 onion, finely grated
- 2 cloves garlic, minced
- 1/2 cup breadcrumbs
- 1/4 cup fresh parsley, finely chopped
- 1/4 cup fresh mint, finely chopped (optional)
- 1 teaspoon dried oregano
- 1 teaspoon ground cumin
- Salt and pepper to taste
- 1 large egg, beaten
- Olive oil for frying

For Serving:

- Tzatziki sauce (optional)
- Lemon wedges
- Fresh parsley, chopped for garnish

Instructions:

1. Prepare Meatball Mixture:

- In a large bowl, combine the ground beef, grated onion, minced garlic, breadcrumbs, chopped parsley, chopped mint (if using), dried oregano, ground cumin, salt, and pepper.

2. Add Beaten Egg:

- Add the beaten egg to the mixture. Mix well until all ingredients are evenly combined.

3. Shape Meatballs:

- With wet hands to prevent sticking, shape the mixture into meatballs of your desired size. Traditionally, keftedes are about the size of a walnut.

4. Heat Olive Oil:

- In a large skillet, heat enough olive oil over medium heat to cover the bottom of the pan.

5. Fry Meatballs:

- Carefully place the meatballs in the hot oil. Cook until browned on all sides and cooked through, about 8-10 minutes. Ensure that they are cooked to an internal temperature of at least 160°F (71°C).

6. Drain Excess Oil:

- Once cooked, transfer the keftedes to a plate lined with paper towels to drain excess oil.

7. Serve:

- Serve the Greek meatballs hot with lemon wedges. Optionally, garnish with chopped fresh parsley.

8. Optional Tzatziki Sauce:

- Serve keftedes with tzatziki sauce on the side for dipping.

9. Enjoy:

- Enjoy the flavorful and juicy keftedes as a main course, appetizer, or part of a Greek meze spread!

Keftedes are a classic Greek dish that brings together the rich flavors of meat, herbs, and spices. They are perfect for sharing with family and friends, especially when served with a side of tzatziki sauce and a squeeze of lemon.

Fasolada (Greek Bean Soup) Recipe

Ingredients:

- 1 cup dried white beans (such as navy beans or Great Northern beans), soaked overnight
- 1/4 cup olive oil
- 1 large onion, finely chopped
- 2 carrots, peeled and diced
- 2 celery stalks, diced
- 3 cloves garlic, minced
- 1 can (14 ounces) diced tomatoes, undrained
- 2 tablespoons tomato paste
- 1 teaspoon dried oregano
- 1 teaspoon dried thyme
- 1 bay leaf
- Salt and pepper to taste
- 4 cups vegetable broth or water
- Fresh parsley, chopped (for garnish)
- Olive oil (for drizzling, optional)
- Crusty bread (for serving)

Instructions:

1. Prepare Dried Beans:

- Rinse and drain the soaked white beans.

2. Sauté Vegetables:

- In a large pot, heat olive oil over medium heat. Add chopped onion, diced carrots, and diced celery. Sauté until the vegetables are softened.

3. Add Garlic and Tomato Paste:

- Add minced garlic to the pot and sauté for an additional minute. Stir in the tomato paste and cook for another 2 minutes.

4. Incorporate Tomatoes and Spices:

- Add the diced tomatoes (with their juice), dried oregano, dried thyme, bay leaf, salt, and pepper to the pot. Stir to combine.

5. Add Soaked Beans:

- Add the soaked and drained white beans to the pot.

6. Pour in Broth or Water:

- Pour in the vegetable broth or water. Bring the mixture to a boil, then reduce the heat to low. Cover and simmer for about 1 to 1.5 hours or until the beans are tender.

7. Check Seasoning:

- Taste and adjust the seasoning, adding more salt and pepper if needed.

8. Serve:

- Ladle the fasolada into bowls. Remove the bay leaf before serving.

9. Garnish and Drizzle:

- Garnish each bowl with chopped fresh parsley. Optionally, drizzle olive oil over the soup for extra richness.

10. Serve with Crusty Bread:

- Serve fasolada hot with crusty bread on the side.

11. Enjoy:

- Enjoy this hearty and nutritious Greek bean soup, a comforting dish that's perfect for cold days!

Fasolada is often considered the national dish of Greece and is known for its simplicity and rich flavors. This bean soup is not only delicious but also a wholesome and satisfying meal.

Greek-Style Hummus with Kalamata Olives Recipe

Ingredients:

- 1 can (15 ounces) chickpeas (garbanzo beans), drained and rinsed
- 1/4 cup tahini
- 1/4 cup extra-virgin olive oil, plus extra for drizzling
- 2 tablespoons fresh lemon juice
- 2 cloves garlic, minced
- 1 teaspoon ground cumin
- 1/2 teaspoon salt, or to taste
- 1/4 teaspoon black pepper
- 1/4 cup Greek yogurt (optional, for creaminess)
- Kalamata olives, pitted and chopped, for garnish
- Fresh parsley, chopped, for garnish
- Paprika, for garnish
- Pita bread or vegetable sticks, for serving

Instructions:

1. Prepare Chickpeas:

- Drain and rinse the chickpeas thoroughly.

2. Blend Hummus:

- In a food processor, combine chickpeas, tahini, olive oil, lemon juice, minced garlic, ground cumin, salt, and black pepper. Blend until smooth and creamy.

3. Add Greek Yogurt (Optional):

- If you prefer a creamier texture, add Greek yogurt to the hummus and blend again until well combined.

4. Adjust Consistency:

- If the hummus is too thick, you can adjust the consistency by adding a bit more olive oil or water and blending until desired thickness is reached.

5. Check Seasoning:

- Taste the hummus and adjust the seasoning, adding more salt or lemon juice if needed.

6. Transfer to Serving Dish:

    - Transfer the hummus to a serving dish, spreading it evenly.

7. Garnish with Olives and Herbs:

    - Sprinkle chopped Kalamata olives, fresh parsley, and a pinch of paprika over the hummus.

8. Drizzle with Olive Oil:

    - Drizzle extra-virgin olive oil over the top for added flavor and richness.

9. Serve:

    - Serve the Greek-style hummus with pita bread or vegetable sticks for dipping.

10. Enjoy:

    - Enjoy this flavorful and Mediterranean-inspired hummus with the rich taste of Kalamata olives as a delicious appetizer or snack!

This Greek-style hummus combines the classic chickpea dip with the bold flavors of Kalamata olives for a delightful twist. It's perfect for serving at gatherings or enjoying as a tasty and healthy snack.

Saganaki (Fried Cheese) Recipe

Ingredients:

- 1 block of firm Greek cheese (such as Kefalotyri or Kasseri), sliced into 1/2-inch thick pieces
- 1/2 cup all-purpose flour, for dredging
- 2 tablespoons olive oil
- 1 lemon, cut into wedges
- 1 tablespoon chopped fresh parsley, for garnish (optional)
- Freshly ground black pepper, to taste

Instructions:

1. Prepare Cheese:

- Slice the firm Greek cheese into approximately 1/2-inch thick pieces.

2. Dredge in Flour:

- Dredge each slice of cheese in all-purpose flour, making sure to coat both sides evenly. Shake off any excess flour.

3. Heat Olive Oil:

- In a non-stick skillet, heat olive oil over medium-high heat.

4. Fry Cheese:

- Place the floured cheese slices in the hot skillet. Fry for about 2-3 minutes on each side or until the cheese develops a golden-brown crust.

5. Serve Hot:

- Transfer the fried cheese to a serving plate while it's hot.

6. Garnish:

- Optionally, sprinkle chopped fresh parsley over the fried cheese for a touch of color.

7. Season with Black Pepper:

- Grind freshly ground black pepper over the saganaki to taste.

8. Serve with Lemon Wedges:

- Serve the saganaki immediately with lemon wedges on the side. The lemon adds a zesty flavor that complements the richness of the cheese.

9. Enjoy:

- Enjoy the saganaki as an appetizer or mezze, and savor the crispy exterior with the gooey, melted cheese inside.

Saganaki, a popular Greek appetizer, is known for its delightful combination of crispy and golden-brown exterior with a warm, gooey interior. This dish is quick to make and makes for an impressive and delicious starter for any meal or gathering.

Greek Salad Skewers Recipe

Ingredients:

- Cherry tomatoes
- Cucumber, cut into chunks
- Kalamata olives, pitted
- Feta cheese, cut into cubes
- Red onion, cut into small wedges
- Extra-virgin olive oil
- Red wine vinegar
- Dried oregano
- Salt and pepper, to taste
- Fresh parsley, chopped (for garnish, optional)
- Wooden skewers

Instructions:

1. Prepare Ingredients:

- Wash and cut the cherry tomatoes, cucumber, feta cheese, and red onion into bite-sized pieces.

2. Assemble Skewers:

- Thread the cherry tomatoes, cucumber chunks, Kalamata olives, feta cheese cubes, and red onion wedges onto wooden skewers in any desired order.

3. Make Greek Salad Dressing:

- In a small bowl, whisk together extra-virgin olive oil, red wine vinegar, dried oregano, salt, and pepper to taste. Adjust the quantities according to your preference.

4. Drizzle Dressing:

- Drizzle the Greek salad dressing over the assembled skewers. Ensure that each ingredient is lightly coated with the dressing.

5. Garnish (Optional):

- Optionally, garnish the skewers with chopped fresh parsley for added freshness and color.

6. Serve:

    - Arrange the Greek salad skewers on a serving platter.

7. Enjoy:

    - Serve these delightful Greek Salad Skewers as a refreshing appetizer, party snack, or a light and healthy side dish. They're perfect for entertaining and sharing the flavors of a classic Greek salad in a convenient and fun-to-eat format!

Moussaka (Eggplant and Meat Casserole) Recipe

Ingredients:

For the Eggplant Layers:

- 2 large eggplants, sliced into 1/2-inch rounds
- Salt
- Olive oil for brushing

For the Meat Sauce:

- 1 pound ground lamb or beef
- 1 large onion, finely chopped
- 3 cloves garlic, minced
- 1 can (14 ounces) diced tomatoes
- 2 tablespoons tomato paste
- 1 teaspoon dried oregano
- 1 teaspoon ground cinnamon
- Salt and black pepper to taste
- Olive oil for cooking

For the Bechamel Sauce:

- 1/2 cup unsalted butter
- 1/2 cup all-purpose flour
- 4 cups milk, warmed
- 1 cup grated Parmesan or Kefalotyri cheese
- 2 large eggs, beaten
- Salt and nutmeg to taste

Instructions:

1. Preheat Oven:

- Preheat the oven to 375°F (190°C).

2. Prepare Eggplant:

- Place the eggplant slices on a baking sheet, sprinkle with salt, and let them sit for about 30 minutes. This helps draw out excess moisture. After 30 minutes, pat the eggplant slices dry with a paper towel and brush both sides with olive oil. Roast the eggplant in the preheated oven for about 20-25 minutes or until golden brown. Set aside.

3. Prepare Meat Sauce:

- In a large skillet, heat olive oil over medium heat. Add chopped onion and cook until softened. Add minced garlic and cook for an additional minute. Add ground lamb or beef and cook until browned. Stir in diced tomatoes, tomato paste, dried oregano, ground cinnamon, salt, and black pepper. Simmer for 15-20 minutes until the sauce thickens.

4. Make Bechamel Sauce:

- In a saucepan, melt butter over medium heat. Stir in flour to create a roux. Gradually whisk in warmed milk until the mixture is smooth and thickened. Remove from heat and stir in grated cheese until melted. Allow the mixture to cool slightly, then whisk in beaten eggs. Season with salt and a pinch of nutmeg.

5. Assemble Moussaka:

- In a greased baking dish, layer half of the roasted eggplant slices. Top with the meat sauce, spreading it evenly. Add another layer of roasted eggplant slices on top. Pour the bechamel sauce over the eggplant, ensuring it covers the entire surface.

6. Bake:

- Bake in the preheated oven for about 45-50 minutes or until the top is golden brown.

7. Cool and Serve:

- Allow the moussaka to cool for a bit before slicing into portions. Serve warm.

8. Enjoy:

- Enjoy this classic Greek Moussaka with layers of flavorful meat sauce, roasted eggplant, and a creamy bechamel sauce! It's a hearty and comforting dish that's perfect for sharing.

Souvlaki (Grilled Meat Skewers) Recipe

Ingredients:

For the Marinade:

- 1.5 pounds (about 700g) boneless meat (chicken, pork, or lamb), cut into bite-sized cubes
- 1/4 cup olive oil
- 3 tablespoons red wine vinegar
- 3 cloves garlic, minced
- 1 teaspoon dried oregano
- 1 teaspoon dried thyme
- 1 teaspoon paprika
- Salt and pepper to taste
- Wooden skewers, soaked in water

For Serving:

- Pita bread
- Tzatziki sauce
- Sliced tomatoes
- Sliced red onions
- Fresh parsley, chopped

Instructions:

1. Prepare Marinade:

- In a bowl, whisk together olive oil, red wine vinegar, minced garlic, dried oregano, dried thyme, paprika, salt, and pepper to create the marinade.

2. Marinate Meat:

- Place the meat cubes in a large, resealable plastic bag or shallow dish. Pour the marinade over the meat, ensuring each piece is well-coated. Seal the bag or cover the dish and refrigerate for at least 2 hours or overnight for better flavor.

3. Skewer Meat:

- Preheat the grill to medium-high heat. Thread the marinated meat cubes onto the soaked wooden skewers.

4. Grill Souvlaki:

- Grill the skewers for about 10-15 minutes, turning occasionally, until the meat is fully cooked and has a nice char.

5. Warm Pita Bread:

- In the last few minutes of grilling, warm the pita bread on the grill.

6. Serve:

- Remove the souvlaki skewers from the grill. Serve the grilled meat on warm pita bread, accompanied by sliced tomatoes, sliced red onions, and a generous dollop of tzatziki sauce.

7. Garnish:

- Garnish the souvlaki with chopped fresh parsley for added freshness.

8. Enjoy:

- Enjoy these delicious and flavorful souvlaki skewers as a classic Greek street food dish! Perfect for a casual meal or gathering.

Yiouvetsi (Baked Orzo with Meat) Recipe

Ingredients:

For the Meat:

- 1.5 pounds (about 700g) lamb or beef, cut into bite-sized cubes
- 2 tablespoons olive oil
- 1 large onion, finely chopped
- 2 cloves garlic, minced
- 1 can (14 ounces) crushed tomatoes
- 1 tablespoon tomato paste
- 1 teaspoon dried oregano
- 1 teaspoon dried thyme
- Salt and pepper to taste

For the Orzo:

- 2 cups orzo pasta
- 4 cups chicken or beef broth (or water)
- 2 tablespoons olive oil
- Salt and pepper to taste

For Baking:

- 1/2 cup grated Parmesan cheese
- Fresh parsley, chopped (for garnish)

Instructions:

1. Preheat Oven:

- Preheat the oven to 375°F (190°C).

2. Cook Meat:

- In a large oven-safe pot or Dutch oven, heat olive oil over medium-high heat. Add the chopped onion and minced garlic, sautéing until softened. Add the meat cubes and brown on all sides.

3. Add Tomatoes and Seasoning:

   - Stir in the crushed tomatoes, tomato paste, dried oregano, dried thyme, salt, and pepper. Simmer for about 10 minutes until the flavors meld together.

4. Cook Orzo:

   - Meanwhile, in a separate pot, bring chicken or beef broth (or water) to a boil. Add the orzo, olive oil, salt, and pepper. Cook the orzo until al dente, as it will continue cooking in the oven.

5. Combine Meat and Orzo:

   - Drain the orzo and add it to the meat mixture in the oven-safe pot. Mix well to combine the flavors.

6. Bake:

   - Sprinkle grated Parmesan cheese over the top. Cover the pot with a lid or foil and transfer it to the preheated oven. Bake for about 30-35 minutes until the orzo is cooked through and has absorbed the flavors.

7. Brown the Top (Optional):

   - If you desire a golden-brown top, uncover the pot for the last 10 minutes of baking.

8. Garnish and Serve:

   - Remove the yiouvetsi from the oven. Garnish with chopped fresh parsley.

9. Enjoy:

   - Serve the yiouvetsi hot as a comforting and flavorful baked orzo dish with meat. Perfect for sharing with family and friends!

Gemista (Stuffed Vegetables) Recipe

Ingredients:

For the Filling:

- 1 cup rice
- 1.5 cups water
- 1 onion, finely chopped
- 2 cloves garlic, minced
- 1/2 cup olive oil
- 1 can (14 ounces) diced tomatoes
- 1/4 cup tomato paste
- 1/4 cup pine nuts (optional)
- 1/4 cup currants or raisins
- 1 teaspoon dried oregano
- 1 teaspoon dried mint
- Salt and pepper to taste
- Fresh parsley, chopped (for garnish)

For the Vegetables:

- 6-8 large tomatoes
- 6-8 bell peppers (green or red)
- 6-8 zucchinis
- Olive oil for drizzling
- Salt and pepper to taste

Instructions:

1. Prepare the Rice:

- Rinse the rice under cold water. In a saucepan, combine the rice and water. Bring to a boil, then reduce heat to low, cover, and simmer until the rice is cooked and water is absorbed (about 15-20 minutes).

2. Sauté Onion and Garlic:

- In a large pan, heat olive oil over medium heat. Sauté finely chopped onion until softened. Add minced garlic and cook for an additional minute.

3. Prepare Filling:

- To the pan, add diced tomatoes, tomato paste, pine nuts (if using), currants or raisins, dried oregano, dried mint, salt, and pepper. Stir in the cooked rice and mix well. Remove from heat and set aside.

4. Prepare Vegetables:

- Cut the tops off the tomatoes and zucchinis. Remove the seeds and pulp from the tomatoes and zucchinis, leaving a shell. Cut the tops off the bell peppers and remove the seeds.

5. Stuff Vegetables:

- Stuff each vegetable with the rice mixture, pressing it down gently. Place the stuffed vegetables in a baking dish.

6. Drizzle with Olive Oil:

- Drizzle the stuffed vegetables with olive oil and season with salt and pepper.

7. Bake:

- Preheat the oven to 375°F (190°C). Cover the baking dish with aluminum foil and bake for about 45-60 minutes or until the vegetables are tender.

8. Garnish and Serve:

- Remove from the oven and garnish with chopped fresh parsley.

9. Enjoy:

- Serve gemista warm, either as a main course or a delightful side dish. These stuffed vegetables are flavorful and nutritious, capturing the essence of Mediterranean cuisine!

Kotopoulo Lemonato (Greek Lemon Chicken) Recipe

Ingredients:

- 4 chicken leg quarters (drumsticks and thighs)
- 1/2 cup olive oil
- 1/2 cup fresh lemon juice
- Zest of 1 lemon
- 4 cloves garlic, minced
- 1 tablespoon dried oregano
- 1 teaspoon dried thyme
- 1 teaspoon dried rosemary
- Salt and black pepper to taste
- 1/2 cup chicken broth
- 1/2 cup white wine (optional)
- Fresh parsley, chopped (for garnish)

Instructions:

1. Marinate the Chicken:

- In a bowl, mix together olive oil, fresh lemon juice, lemon zest, minced garlic, dried oregano, dried thyme, dried rosemary, salt, and black pepper to create the marinade.

2. Coat Chicken:

- Place the chicken leg quarters in a large resealable plastic bag or a shallow dish. Pour the marinade over the chicken, making sure each piece is well-coated. Seal the bag or cover the dish and refrigerate for at least 2 hours, preferably overnight for better flavor.

3. Preheat Oven:

- Preheat the oven to 375°F (190°C).

4. Arrange Chicken in Baking Dish:

- Place the marinated chicken leg quarters in a baking dish.

5. Add Liquid:

- In a small bowl, mix together chicken broth and white wine (if using). Pour this mixture around the chicken in the baking dish.

6. Bake:

    - Bake the chicken in the preheated oven for about 45-60 minutes or until the chicken is cooked through, and the skin is golden brown and crispy.

7. Baste Chicken:

    - Baste the chicken with the pan juices every 20-30 minutes to keep it moist.

8. Check Internal Temperature:

    - Ensure the chicken reaches a safe internal temperature of 165°F (74°C).

9. Garnish and Serve:

    - Remove the chicken from the oven, garnish with chopped fresh parsley, and serve hot.

10. Enjoy:

    - Enjoy this flavorful and zesty Greek Lemon Chicken with your favorite side dishes. The combination of lemon and herbs makes it a delightful and classic Greek dish!

Psari Plaki (Baked Fish) Recipe

Ingredients:

- 4 fish fillets (such as cod or sea bass)
- 1/4 cup olive oil
- 1 onion, thinly sliced
- 2 cloves garlic, minced
- 1 can (14 ounces) diced tomatoes
- 1/4 cup tomato paste
- 1/4 cup dry white wine
- 1 teaspoon dried oregano
- 1 teaspoon dried thyme
- 1 teaspoon paprika
- Salt and black pepper to taste
- 1/2 cup Kalamata olives, pitted and sliced
- 1/4 cup capers, drained
- Fresh parsley, chopped (for garnish)
- Lemon wedges (for serving)

Instructions:

1. Preheat Oven:

- Preheat the oven to 375°F (190°C).

2. Sauté Onion and Garlic:

- In a skillet, heat olive oil over medium heat. Add thinly sliced onion and cook until softened. Add minced garlic and sauté for an additional minute.

3. Prepare Tomato Sauce:

- Stir in diced tomatoes, tomato paste, white wine, dried oregano, dried thyme, paprika, salt, and black pepper. Simmer for about 10 minutes until the sauce thickens.

4. Assemble Baking Dish:

- Place the fish fillets in a greased baking dish. Pour the tomato sauce over the fish, ensuring it is well-coated.

5. Add Olives and Capers:

- Sprinkle sliced Kalamata olives and drained capers over the fish and tomato sauce.

6. Bake:

- Bake in the preheated oven for about 20-25 minutes or until the fish is cooked through and flakes easily with a fork.

7. Check Internal Temperature:

- Ensure the fish reaches a safe internal temperature of 145°F (63°C).

8. Garnish and Serve:

- Remove the baked fish from the oven. Garnish with chopped fresh parsley.

9. Serve with Lemon Wedges:

- Serve the Psari Plaki hot, with lemon wedges on the side for squeezing over the fish.

10. Enjoy:

- Enjoy this delicious and Mediterranean-inspired Psari Plaki, a flavorful baked fish dish that captures the essence of Greek cuisine!

Keftethes me Saltsa Domata (Meatballs in Tomato Sauce) Recipe

Ingredients:

For the Meatballs (Keftethes):

- 1 pound ground beef or a mixture of beef and pork
- 1/2 cup breadcrumbs
- 1 onion, finely chopped
- 2 cloves garlic, minced
- 1/4 cup fresh parsley, chopped
- 1 teaspoon dried oregano
- 1 teaspoon dried mint
- Salt and pepper to taste
- 1 egg, beaten
- Olive oil for frying

For the Tomato Sauce (Saltsa Domata):

- 1 can (14 ounces) crushed tomatoes
- 1 onion, finely chopped
- 2 cloves garlic, minced
- 1 teaspoon dried oregano
- 1 teaspoon dried basil
- Salt and pepper to taste
- 1/4 cup fresh parsley, chopped (for garnish)

Instructions:

1. Prepare the Meatballs:

- In a large bowl, combine ground beef, breadcrumbs, finely chopped onion, minced garlic, chopped fresh parsley, dried oregano, dried mint, salt, pepper, and the beaten egg. Mix until well combined.

2. Shape the Meatballs:

- With wet hands to prevent sticking, shape the mixture into meatballs of your desired size.

3. Fry the Meatballs:

    - In a skillet, heat olive oil over medium-high heat. Fry the meatballs until browned on all sides. Once browned, remove them from the skillet and set aside.

4. Prepare the Tomato Sauce:

    - In the same skillet, add finely chopped onion and minced garlic. Sauté until the onion is softened. Add crushed tomatoes, dried oregano, dried basil, salt, and pepper. Simmer for about 10-15 minutes until the sauce thickens.

5. Add Meatballs to the Sauce:

    - Return the browned meatballs to the skillet, coating them with the tomato sauce. Simmer for an additional 10-15 minutes, allowing the flavors to meld.

6. Check Meatballs:

    - Ensure the meatballs are cooked through by cutting one open to check the center.

7. Garnish and Serve:

    - Garnish with chopped fresh parsley.

8. Enjoy:

    - Serve the Keftethes me Saltsa Domata hot over rice, pasta, or with crusty bread. Enjoy this classic Greek dish that combines flavorful meatballs with a rich tomato sauce!

Arni Lemonato (Lamb in Lemon Sauce) Recipe

Ingredients:

- 2.5 to 3 pounds lamb, cut into chunks (shoulder or leg)
- 1/2 cup olive oil
- 1 large onion, finely chopped
- 4 cloves garlic, minced
- 1 cup chicken broth
- 1/2 cup dry white wine
- Juice of 2 lemons
- 1 teaspoon dried oregano
- 1 teaspoon dried thyme
- Salt and black pepper to taste
- 2 bay leaves
- 1 tablespoon all-purpose flour (optional, for thickening)
- Fresh parsley, chopped (for garnish)

Instructions:

1. Preheat Oven:

   - Preheat the oven to 350°F (175°C).

2. Sear the Lamb:

   - In a large oven-safe pot or Dutch oven, heat olive oil over medium-high heat. Sear the lamb chunks until browned on all sides.

3. Sauté Onion and Garlic:

   - Add finely chopped onion and minced garlic to the pot. Sauté until the onion is softened.

4. Deglaze with Wine:

   - Pour in the dry white wine to deglaze the pot, scraping up any browned bits from the bottom.

5. Add Broth and Lemon Juice:

- Add chicken broth, lemon juice, dried oregano, dried thyme, salt, black pepper, and bay leaves. Stir to combine.

6. Braise in the Oven:

    - Cover the pot and transfer it to the preheated oven. Braise the lamb for about 2 to 2.5 hours or until the meat is tender and falls off the bone.

7. Optional Thickening:

    - If you desire a thicker sauce, mix 1 tablespoon of all-purpose flour with a little water to make a paste. Stir the paste into the pot during the last 30 minutes of cooking.

8. Check Seasoning:

    - Taste and adjust the seasoning if necessary.

9. Garnish and Serve:

    - Remove the pot from the oven and discard the bay leaves. Garnish with chopped fresh parsley.

10. Enjoy:

    - Serve Arni Lemonato hot over rice, potatoes, or with your favorite side dishes. The lemon-infused lamb with aromatic herbs creates a delightful Greek dish!

Garides Saganaki (Shrimp in Tomato and Feta Sauce) Recipe

Ingredients:

- 1 pound large shrimp, peeled and deveined
- 2 tablespoons olive oil
- 1 onion, finely chopped
- 3 cloves garlic, minced
- 1 can (14 ounces) diced tomatoes
- 1/4 cup tomato paste
- 1/2 cup dry white wine
- 1 teaspoon dried oregano
- 1 teaspoon dried thyme
- Salt and black pepper to taste
- Pinch of red pepper flakes (optional)
- 1 cup feta cheese, crumbled
- Fresh parsley, chopped (for garnish)
- Crusty bread, for serving

Instructions:

1. Preheat Oven:

- Preheat the oven to 375°F (190°C).

2. Sauté Onion and Garlic:

- In an oven-safe skillet, heat olive oil over medium heat. Add finely chopped onion and minced garlic. Sauté until the onion is softened.

3. Add Tomatoes and Tomato Paste:

- Stir in diced tomatoes, tomato paste, dry white wine, dried oregano, dried thyme, salt, black pepper, and red pepper flakes if using. Simmer for about 10 minutes until the sauce thickens.

4. Cook Shrimp:

- Add the peeled and deveined shrimp to the skillet. Cook for 2-3 minutes, just until the shrimp start turning pink.

5. Add Feta Cheese:

- Sprinkle crumbled feta cheese over the top of the shrimp and tomato mixture.

6. Bake in the Oven:

- Transfer the skillet to the preheated oven and bake for about 15-20 minutes, or until the shrimp are fully cooked, and the feta cheese is melted and slightly golden.

7. Garnish:

- Remove from the oven and garnish with chopped fresh parsley.

8. Serve:

- Serve the Garides Saganaki hot, straight from the skillet, with crusty bread for dipping.

9. Enjoy:

- Enjoy this flavorful Garides Saganaki as a delicious appetizer or main dish. The combination of shrimp, tomatoes, and feta creates a rich and satisfying Greek dish!

Gigantes Plaki (Baked Giant Beans) Recipe

Ingredients:

For the Giant Beans:

- 2 cups dried giant beans (or lima beans), soaked overnight
- Water for cooking beans
- 1 onion, finely chopped
- 2 cloves garlic, minced
- 1/4 cup olive oil
- 1 can (14 ounces) diced tomatoes
- 1/4 cup tomato paste
- 1 teaspoon dried oregano
- 1 teaspoon dried thyme
- Salt and black pepper to taste
- 1 cup vegetable broth or water
- 2 bay leaves

For the Topping:

- 1/4 cup olive oil
- 1 tablespoon fresh parsley, chopped
- 1 tablespoon fresh dill, chopped
- 1 lemon, zested
- Salt and black pepper to taste

Instructions:

1. Cook Giant Beans:

- Drain the soaked giant beans and place them in a large pot. Cover with fresh water and bring to a boil. Reduce heat to low and simmer for about 45 minutes to 1 hour, or until the beans are tender. Drain and set aside.

2. Preheat Oven:

- Preheat the oven to 375°F (190°C).

3. Sauté Onion and Garlic:

- In a large oven-safe pot or Dutch oven, heat 1/4 cup olive oil over medium heat. Add finely chopped onion and minced garlic. Sauté until the onion is softened.

4. Prepare Tomato Sauce:

    - Stir in diced tomatoes, tomato paste, dried oregano, dried thyme, salt, and black pepper. Cook for about 5 minutes until the mixture thickens.

5. Add Cooked Beans:

    - Add the cooked giant beans to the pot, stirring to coat them in the tomato sauce.

6. Add Broth and Bay Leaves:

    - Pour in vegetable broth (or water) and add bay leaves. Stir well.

7. Bake in the Oven:

    - Cover the pot with a lid or foil and transfer it to the preheated oven. Bake for about 45-60 minutes, allowing the flavors to meld.

8. Prepare Topping:

    - In a small bowl, mix together 1/4 cup olive oil, chopped fresh parsley, chopped fresh dill, lemon zest, salt, and black pepper.

9. Serve:

    - Remove the pot from the oven. Drizzle the olive oil and herb topping over the baked giant beans.

10. Enjoy:

    - Serve Gigantes Plaki hot as a satisfying and flavorful Greek dish. Enjoy it as a main course or a delightful side dish!

Horta Vrasta (Boiled Greens) Recipe

Ingredients:

- 1 pound mixed greens (such as dandelion greens, mustard greens, chicory, or spinach)
- Water for boiling
- Salt to taste
- Extra-virgin olive oil for drizzling
- Lemon wedges for serving (optional)

Instructions:

1. Prepare Greens:

- Wash the greens thoroughly under running water to remove any dirt or debris.

2. Boil Water:

- Fill a large pot with water and bring it to a boil.

3. Boil Greens:

- Add the washed greens to the boiling water. If using a mix of greens, add the tougher ones first and the more delicate ones later. Boil the greens for about 5-10 minutes or until they are tender.

4. Drain and Cool:

- Once the greens are tender, drain them in a colander and rinse with cold water to stop the cooking process. Allow them to cool for a few minutes.

5. Season with Salt:

- Place the boiled greens in a serving dish and season with salt to taste.

6. Drizzle with Olive Oil:

- Drizzle extra-virgin olive oil over the boiled greens. Use a good quality olive oil for enhanced flavor.

7. Serve:

- Serve the Horta Vrasta either warm or at room temperature. Optionally, provide lemon wedges on the side for those who prefer a citrusy flavor.

8. Enjoy:

- Enjoy this simple and nutritious dish as a side to your main meal. Horta Vrasta is a traditional Greek way of preparing greens, emphasizing their natural flavors and the health benefits they offer.

Spanakorizo (Spinach and Rice) Recipe

Ingredients:

- 1 cup long-grain white rice
- 2 tablespoons olive oil
- 1 onion, finely chopped
- 2 cloves garlic, minced
- 1 pound fresh spinach, washed and chopped
- 1 can (14 ounces) diced tomatoes
- 1 teaspoon tomato paste
- 1 teaspoon dried dill
- 1 teaspoon dried oregano
- Salt and black pepper to taste
- 2 cups vegetable broth or water
- Juice of 1 lemon
- Crumbled feta cheese for garnish (optional)

Instructions:

1. Rinse Rice:

- Rinse the rice under cold water and set it aside.

2. Sauté Onion and Garlic:

- In a large pot or deep skillet, heat olive oil over medium heat. Add finely chopped onion and minced garlic. Sauté until the onion is translucent.

3. Add Spinach:

- Add the chopped spinach to the pot. Stir and cook until the spinach is wilted.

4. Incorporate Tomatoes and Paste:

- Stir in diced tomatoes, tomato paste, dried dill, dried oregano, salt, and black pepper. Cook for a few minutes to allow the flavors to meld.

5. Add Rice:

- Add the rinsed rice to the pot and mix well with the other ingredients.

6. Pour Broth and Lemon Juice:

    - Pour in vegetable broth (or water) and add the juice of one lemon. Stir to combine.

7. Simmer:

    - Bring the mixture to a boil, then reduce the heat to low. Cover the pot and let it simmer for about 15-20 minutes or until the rice is cooked and has absorbed the liquid.

8. Check for Seasoning:

    - Taste and adjust the seasoning if necessary.

9. Serve:

    - Spoon the Spanakorizo onto serving plates. Optionally, garnish with crumbled feta cheese.

10. Enjoy:

    - Enjoy this comforting and flavorful Spanakorizo as a delicious main dish or side. The combination of spinach, rice, and Mediterranean herbs makes it a classic and nutritious Greek dish!

Fasolakia (Greek Green Beans) Recipe

Ingredients:

- 1 pound fresh green beans, ends trimmed and cut into bite-sized pieces
- 2 tablespoons olive oil
- 1 onion, finely chopped
- 2 cloves garlic, minced
- 1 can (14 ounces) diced tomatoes
- 1 teaspoon tomato paste
- 1 teaspoon dried oregano
- 1 teaspoon dried mint
- Salt and black pepper to taste
- 1 cup vegetable broth or water
- 1 tablespoon fresh parsley, chopped (for garnish)
- Lemon wedges for serving (optional)

Instructions:

1. Prepare Green Beans:

- Trim the ends of the fresh green beans and cut them into bite-sized pieces.

2. Sauté Onion and Garlic:

- In a large pot or deep skillet, heat olive oil over medium heat. Add finely chopped onion and minced garlic. Sauté until the onion is softened.

3. Add Tomatoes and Paste:

- Stir in diced tomatoes, tomato paste, dried oregano, dried mint, salt, and black pepper. Cook for a few minutes until the tomatoes break down.

4. Incorporate Green Beans:

- Add the green beans to the pot and coat them in the tomato mixture.

5. Pour Broth:

- Pour in vegetable broth (or water) and bring the mixture to a simmer.

6. Simmer:

   - Cover the pot and let the Fasolakia simmer for about 20-25 minutes or until the green beans are tender.

7. Check for Seasoning:

   - Taste and adjust the seasoning if necessary.

8. Garnish:

   - Sprinkle chopped fresh parsley over the Fasolakia.

9. Serve:

   - Serve the Greek Green Beans hot as a flavorful side dish.

10. Enjoy:

    - Enjoy Fasolakia on its own or alongside your favorite main course. Optionally, serve with lemon wedges for a burst of citrus flavor. This dish captures the simplicity and deliciousness of Greek cuisine!

Revithia (Chickpea Soup) Recipe

Ingredients:

- 1 cup dried chickpeas, soaked overnight
- 2 tablespoons olive oil
- 1 onion, finely chopped
- 2 cloves garlic, minced
- 1 carrot, diced
- 2 celery stalks, diced
- 1 potato, peeled and diced
- 1 teaspoon ground cumin
- 1 teaspoon ground coriander
- 1 teaspoon paprika
- Salt and black pepper to taste
- 1 can (14 ounces) diced tomatoes
- 6 cups vegetable broth
- Fresh parsley, chopped (for garnish)
- Lemon wedges for serving (optional)

Instructions:

1. Prepare Chickpeas:

- Rinse and drain the soaked chickpeas.

2. Sauté Onion and Garlic:

- In a large pot, heat olive oil over medium heat. Add finely chopped onion and minced garlic. Sauté until the onion is softened.

3. Add Vegetables:

- Add diced carrot, diced celery, and diced potato to the pot. Cook for a few minutes until the vegetables start to soften.

4. Spice it Up:

- Stir in ground cumin, ground coriander, paprika, salt, and black pepper. Mix well to coat the vegetables in the spices.

5. Add Chickpeas:

- Add the soaked and drained chickpeas to the pot. Stir to combine with the vegetables and spices.

6. Pour in Broth:

- Pour in vegetable broth, ensuring that the chickpeas and vegetables are fully submerged.

7. Simmer:

- Bring the soup to a boil, then reduce the heat to low. Cover the pot and let it simmer for about 1.5 to 2 hours or until the chickpeas are tender.

8. Add Tomatoes:

- Stir in diced tomatoes and continue to simmer for an additional 15-20 minutes.

9. Check for Seasoning:

- Taste and adjust the seasoning if necessary.

10. Garnish and Serve:

- Ladle the Revithia into bowls, garnish with chopped fresh parsley, and optionally serve with lemon wedges on the side.

11. Enjoy:

- Enjoy this hearty and nutritious Revithia (Chickpea Soup) hot, especially on a cold day. It's a comforting dish with a blend of flavors and spices that make it a staple in Greek cuisine.

Kolokithokeftedes (Zucchini Fritters) Recipe

Ingredients:

- 2 medium zucchinis, grated
- 1 teaspoon salt (for draining excess moisture from zucchini)
- 1/2 cup feta cheese, crumbled
- 1/4 cup fresh mint, finely chopped
- 1/4 cup fresh dill, finely chopped
- 3 green onions, finely chopped
- 2 cloves garlic, minced
- 1 cup breadcrumbs
- 2 eggs, beaten
- Salt and black pepper to taste
- Olive oil for frying
- Greek yogurt or tzatziki sauce (for serving)

Instructions:

1. Grate and Drain Zucchini:

- Grate the zucchinis and place them in a colander. Sprinkle with 1 teaspoon of salt and let them sit for about 15 minutes to release excess moisture. Afterward, squeeze and drain the grated zucchini using a clean kitchen towel.

2. Prepare Zucchini Mixture:

- In a large mixing bowl, combine the drained zucchini, crumbled feta cheese, chopped mint, chopped dill, chopped green onions, minced garlic, breadcrumbs, beaten eggs, salt, and black pepper. Mix well until all ingredients are combined.

3. Form Patties:

- Take small portions of the mixture and shape them into patties or fritters.

4. Heat Olive Oil:

- In a skillet, heat olive oil over medium-high heat.

5. Fry the Fritters:

- Carefully place the zucchini fritters in the hot oil. Fry them for about 3-4 minutes on each side or until they are golden brown and cooked through.

6. Drain Excess Oil:

- Place the cooked fritters on a plate lined with paper towels to absorb any excess oil.

7. Serve:

- Serve the Kolokithokeftedes hot, with a side of Greek yogurt or tzatziki sauce for dipping.

8. Enjoy:

- Enjoy these crispy and flavorful Zucchini Fritters as a tasty appetizer or side dish. They are a delightful way to incorporate zucchini into your meals, Greek-style!

Riganada (Greek Bread Salad) Recipe

Ingredients:

- 1 loaf of rustic country bread, preferably day-old, cut into bite-sized cubes
- 4 large tomatoes, diced
- 1 cucumber, diced
- 1 red onion, thinly sliced
- Kalamata olives, pitted and sliced (to taste)
- Feta cheese, crumbled (to taste)
- Fresh oregano or dried oregano (to taste)
- Salt and black pepper to taste
- Extra-virgin olive oil
- Red wine vinegar
- Optional: Capers for added flavor

Instructions:

1. Prepare Bread Cubes:

- Cut the rustic country bread into bite-sized cubes. If the bread is not day-old, you can toast the cubes in the oven until they become slightly crisp.

2. Assemble Salad:

- In a large mixing bowl, combine the diced tomatoes, diced cucumber, thinly sliced red onion, Kalamata olives, and crumbled feta cheese.

3. Add Bread Cubes:

- Add the bite-sized bread cubes to the bowl. Toss the salad gently to combine.

4. Season:

- Season the salad with fresh oregano or dried oregano, salt, and black pepper. Adjust the quantities based on your taste preferences.

5. Dress the Salad:

- Drizzle extra-virgin olive oil and red wine vinegar over the salad. Toss again to ensure even coating. Adjust the dressing quantities to achieve your desired level of moisture.

6. Optional Ingredients:

- If you like, add capers for an extra burst of flavor. Adjust the amount based on your preference.

7. Let it Sit:

- Allow the salad to sit for a few minutes to allow the bread to absorb the flavors.

8. Serve:

- Serve Riganada immediately, allowing the bread to retain some of its crunchiness.

9. Enjoy:

- Enjoy this delightful and refreshing Greek Bread Salad as a light meal or a flavorful side dish. It's a perfect representation of Greek cuisine's emphasis on fresh and vibrant ingredients.

Briam (Greek Ratatouille) Recipe

Ingredients:

- 3 medium-sized potatoes, peeled and sliced
- 3 medium-sized zucchinis, sliced
- 3 eggplants, sliced
- 3 bell peppers (assorted colors), sliced
- 4 large tomatoes, sliced
- 1 large red onion, thinly sliced
- 4 cloves garlic, minced
- 1/2 cup fresh parsley, chopped
- 1/2 cup fresh mint, chopped
- Salt and black pepper to taste
- 1 teaspoon dried oregano
- 1/2 cup olive oil
- 1 cup tomato sauce or crushed tomatoes
- Optional: Feta cheese for serving

Instructions:

1. Prepare Vegetables:

- Preheat the oven to 375°F (190°C). Slice the potatoes, zucchinis, eggplants, bell peppers, and tomatoes into uniform thickness.

2. Assemble in Layers:

- In a large baking dish, layer the sliced vegetables, alternating between potatoes, zucchinis, eggplants, bell peppers, tomatoes, and red onions. Repeat until all vegetables are used.

3. Season:

- Sprinkle minced garlic, chopped fresh parsley, chopped fresh mint, salt, black pepper, and dried oregano evenly over the layered vegetables.

4. Drizzle Olive Oil:

- Drizzle olive oil generously over the entire dish.

5. Add Tomato Sauce:

   - Pour tomato sauce or crushed tomatoes over the vegetables, ensuring it spreads evenly.

6. Toss and Coat:

   - Gently toss the vegetables to coat them in the seasonings, herbs, and tomato sauce.

7. Bake:

   - Cover the baking dish with aluminum foil and bake in the preheated oven for approximately 1 to 1.5 hours, or until the vegetables are tender.

8. Check for Doneness:

   - Check the doneness by inserting a fork into the potatoes. They should be soft and easily pierced.

9. Optional: Broil for Crispy Top (if desired):

   - If you prefer a crispy top, uncover the baking dish and broil for a few minutes until the top is golden brown.

10. Serve:

    - Serve Briam warm as a main course or a hearty side dish.

11. Optional: Feta Cheese Garnish:

    - Optionally, garnish with crumbled feta cheese before serving.

12. Enjoy:

    - Enjoy this delicious and wholesome Greek Ratatouille, known as Briam. It's a flavorful medley of Mediterranean vegetables that captures the essence of Greek cuisine.

Manestra (Greek Orzo Pasta) Recipe

Ingredients:

- 1 cup orzo pasta
- 2 tablespoons olive oil
- 1 onion, finely chopped
- 2 cloves garlic, minced
- 1 can (14 ounces) diced tomatoes
- 1 tablespoon tomato paste
- 1 teaspoon dried oregano
- 1 teaspoon dried thyme
- Salt and black pepper to taste
- 4 cups vegetable or chicken broth
- Fresh parsley, chopped (for garnish)
- Grated Parmesan cheese (optional, for serving)

Instructions:

1. Sauté Onion and Garlic:

- In a pot or deep skillet, heat olive oil over medium heat. Add finely chopped onion and minced garlic. Sauté until the onion is softened.

2. Add Tomatoes and Paste:

- Stir in diced tomatoes, tomato paste, dried oregano, dried thyme, salt, and black pepper. Cook for a few minutes until the tomatoes break down.

3. Incorporate Orzo:

- Add the orzo pasta to the pot and coat it in the tomato mixture.

4. Pour in Broth:

- Pour in vegetable or chicken broth, ensuring that the orzo is fully submerged.

5. Simmer:

- Bring the mixture to a boil, then reduce the heat to low. Cover the pot and let it simmer for about 10-12 minutes, or until the orzo is cooked and has absorbed most of the liquid. Stir occasionally to prevent sticking.

6. Check for Seasoning:

- Taste and adjust the seasoning if necessary.

7. Garnish:

- Garnish the Manestra with chopped fresh parsley.

8. Serve:

- Serve the Greek Orzo Pasta hot as a flavorful side dish or light main course.

9. Optional: Parmesan Cheese:

- Optionally, sprinkle grated Parmesan cheese over the Manestra before serving.

10. Enjoy:

- Enjoy this comforting and delicious Manestra, a Greek-style orzo pasta dish that's simple to prepare and bursting with Mediterranean flavors!

Patates Lemonates (Lemon Potatoes) Recipe

Ingredients:

- 4 large potatoes, peeled and cut into wedges or chunks
- 1/2 cup olive oil
- 1/2 cup fresh lemon juice
- 4 cloves garlic, minced
- 1 teaspoon dried oregano
- Salt and black pepper to taste
- 1 cup vegetable or chicken broth
- Fresh parsley, chopped (for garnish)
- Lemon slices (for garnish)

Instructions:

1. Preheat Oven:

- Preheat the oven to 400°F (200°C).

2. Prepare Potatoes:

- Peel the potatoes and cut them into wedges or chunks, depending on your preference.

3. Mix Marinade:

- In a bowl, mix together olive oil, fresh lemon juice, minced garlic, dried oregano, salt, and black pepper. This will be your marinade.

4. Coat Potatoes:

- Place the potato wedges in a large baking dish. Pour the marinade over the potatoes, ensuring they are well-coated.

5. Add Broth:

- Pour vegetable or chicken broth into the baking dish. The broth will help keep the potatoes moist and flavorful.

6. Bake:

- Bake in the preheated oven for about 45-55 minutes or until the potatoes are tender and golden brown. Toss the potatoes occasionally to coat them in the marinade and broth.

7. Check for Doneness:

- Check for doneness by inserting a fork into the potatoes. They should be soft on the inside.

8. Garnish:

- Once done, remove from the oven and garnish with chopped fresh parsley and lemon slices.

9. Serve:

- Serve Patates Lemonates hot as a delicious side dish.

10. Enjoy:

    - Enjoy these zesty and flavorful Lemon Potatoes that are a classic Greek side dish. They pair well with a variety of main courses and bring a burst of citrusy goodness to your meal!

Baklava (Phyllo and Nut Pastry) Recipe

Ingredients:

For the Filling:

- 2 cups mixed nuts (walnuts, pistachios, almonds), finely chopped
- 1/2 cup sugar
- 1 teaspoon ground cinnamon

For the Phyllo Layers:

- 1 pound (about 40 sheets) phyllo dough, thawed if frozen
- 1 cup unsalted butter, melted

For the Syrup:

- 1 cup water
- 1 cup sugar
- 1/2 cup honey
- 1 cinnamon stick
- 3 whole cloves
- 1 teaspoon vanilla extract
- Zest of 1 lemon

Instructions:

1. Prepare the Filling:

- In a bowl, mix together the finely chopped mixed nuts, sugar, and ground cinnamon. Set aside.

2. Preheat Oven:

- Preheat your oven to 350°F (175°C).

3. Prepare Phyllo Layers:

- Brush a baking dish (usually 9x13 inches) with melted butter. Place a sheet of phyllo dough in the dish, brush with butter, and repeat until you have about 10 layers.

4. Add Nut Filling:

- Spread a portion of the nut filling evenly over the phyllo layers.

5. Layer Phyllo Again:

- Place another layer of phyllo dough on top of the nut filling, brush with butter, and repeat until you've used about 10 layers.

6. Continue Layering:

- Repeat the process of adding nut filling and layering phyllo dough until all the nut filling is used, finishing with a top layer of phyllo dough.

7. Cut into Diamond Shapes:

- With a sharp knife, carefully cut the baklava into diamond shapes. This can be achieved by cutting diagonally across the pan and then making straight cuts perpendicular to the first ones.

8. Bake:

- Place the baklava in the preheated oven and bake for about 45-50 minutes or until golden brown.

9. Prepare the Syrup:

- While the baklava is baking, combine water, sugar, honey, cinnamon stick, cloves, vanilla extract, and lemon zest in a saucepan. Bring the mixture to a boil, then reduce heat and simmer for 10-15 minutes. Remove the cinnamon stick and cloves.

10. Pour Syrup Over Hot Baklava:

- Once the baklava is out of the oven and still hot, immediately pour the cooled syrup evenly over the hot pastry.

11. Allow to Cool:

- Allow the baklava to cool completely before serving. This allows the phyllo layers to absorb the syrup.

12. Enjoy:

- Serve and enjoy this sweet and nutty Baklava! It's a delightful treat with layers of crispy phyllo and a honey-infused nut filling.

Galaktoboureko (Custard Pastry) Recipe

Ingredients:

For the Filling:

- 4 cups whole milk
- 1 cup fine semolina flour
- 1 cup sugar
- 4 large eggs
- 1 teaspoon vanilla extract
- Zest of 1 lemon

For the Phyllo Layers:

- 1 pound (about 40 sheets) phyllo dough, thawed if frozen
- 1 cup unsalted butter, melted

For the Syrup:

- 2 cups water
- 2 cups sugar
- 1 lemon, juiced

Instructions:

1. Prepare the Custard Filling:

- In a saucepan, heat the milk over medium heat until it's warm but not boiling. In a separate bowl, whisk together semolina flour, sugar, eggs, vanilla extract, and lemon zest. Gradually add the warm milk, whisking continuously.

2. Cook Custard:

- Place the saucepan back on the heat and continue to cook the custard mixture, stirring constantly, until it thickens to a pudding-like consistency. Remove from heat and let it cool.

3. Preheat Oven:

- Preheat your oven to 350°F (175°C).

4. Prepare Phyllo Layers:

    - Brush a baking dish (usually 9x13 inches) with melted butter. Place a sheet of phyllo dough in the dish, brush with butter, and repeat until you have about 10 layers.

5. Add Custard Filling:

    - Spread the cooled custard filling evenly over the phyllo layers.

6. Layer Phyllo Again:

    - Place another layer of phyllo dough on top of the custard, brush with butter, and repeat until you've used about 10 layers.

7. Continue Layering:

    - Repeat the process of layering phyllo dough and brushing with butter until all the custard filling is covered, finishing with a top layer of phyllo dough.

8. Cut into Diamond Shapes:

    - With a sharp knife, carefully cut the galaktoboureko into diamond shapes.

9. Bake:

    - Place the pastry in the preheated oven and bake for about 45-50 minutes or until the top is golden brown.

10. Prepare the Syrup:

    - While the galaktoboureko is baking, prepare the syrup. In a saucepan, combine water, sugar, and lemon juice. Bring to a boil, then reduce heat and simmer for 10-15 minutes. Remove from heat and let it cool.

11. Pour Syrup Over Hot Pastry:

- Once the galaktoboureko is out of the oven and still hot, immediately pour the cooled syrup evenly over the hot pastry.

12. Allow to Cool:

- Allow the galaktoboureko to cool completely before serving. This allows the phyllo layers to absorb the syrup.

13. Enjoy:

- Serve and enjoy this classic Greek dessert with its creamy custard filling and crispy phyllo layers!

Loukoumades (Honey Puffs) Recipe

Ingredients:

For the Dough:

- 2 cups all-purpose flour
- 1 ½ teaspoons active dry yeast
- 1 teaspoon sugar
- ½ teaspoon salt
- 1 ½ cups warm water

For Frying:

- Vegetable oil for deep frying

For Syrup:

- 1 cup honey
- 1 cup water
- Optional: Cinnamon sticks or orange peel for flavor

For Topping:

- Chopped nuts (e.g., walnuts or pistachios)
- Cinnamon (optional)

Instructions:

1. Prepare Dough:

- In a bowl, combine the warm water, sugar, and active dry yeast. Let it sit for about 5-10 minutes until it becomes frothy.

2. Mix Dough Ingredients:

- In a large mixing bowl, combine the flour and salt. Pour in the yeast mixture and mix until you have a smooth, sticky batter. Cover the bowl with a kitchen towel and let the dough rise in a warm place for about 1-2 hours or until it doubles in size.

3. Heat Oil:

   - Heat vegetable oil in a deep fryer or a deep, heavy-bottomed pot to 350°F (175°C).

4. Form and Fry Loukoumades:

   - Wet your hands and scoop up a small amount of dough. Drop it into the hot oil, shaping it into a round puff using a spoon or your wet hands. Fry until golden brown, turning them occasionally to ensure even cooking. Remove them with a slotted spoon and place them on paper towels to absorb excess oil.

5. Prepare Syrup:

   - In a saucepan, combine honey, water, and optional cinnamon sticks or orange peel. Bring to a simmer and let it cook for about 5-10 minutes. Remove from heat and let it cool slightly.

6. Coat Loukoumades in Syrup:

   - Dip the fried loukoumades into the warm syrup, making sure to coat them evenly. Allow them to soak for a few seconds before removing.

7. Serve and Garnish:

   - Arrange the loukoumades on a serving plate. Optionally, sprinkle chopped nuts and cinnamon on top.

8. Enjoy:

   - Serve these delicious honey puffs immediately, while they are still warm and dripping with syrup. Loukoumades are a delightful treat, often enjoyed during festive occasions and celebrations in Greek cuisine.

Koulourakia (Butter Cookies) Recipe

Ingredients:

- 1 cup unsalted butter, softened
- 1 cup granulated sugar
- 3 large eggs
- 1 teaspoon vanilla extract
- 1/2 cup milk
- 4 to 4 1/2 cups all-purpose flour
- 2 teaspoons baking powder
- 1/2 teaspoon salt
- Sesame seeds for coating

Instructions:

1. Preheat Oven:

    - Preheat your oven to 350°F (175°C). Line baking sheets with parchment paper.

2. Cream Butter and Sugar:

    - In a large mixing bowl, cream together the softened butter and sugar until light and fluffy.

3. Add Eggs and Vanilla:

    - Add the eggs one at a time, beating well after each addition. Mix in the vanilla extract.

4. Combine Dry Ingredients:

    - In a separate bowl, whisk together the flour, baking powder, and salt.

5. Alternately Add Dry Ingredients and Milk:

    - Gradually add the dry ingredients to the butter mixture, alternating with the milk. Start and finish with the dry ingredients. Mix until just combined.

6. Shape Cookies:

- Take a small portion of the dough and roll it into a rope about 5 inches long. Twist the rope into a braid or circle shape. Place the shaped cookies on the prepared baking sheets, leaving some space between each.

7. Coat with Sesame Seeds:

- Brush each cookie with a little milk and sprinkle sesame seeds on top, pressing them gently into the dough.

8. Bake:

- Bake in the preheated oven for about 12-15 minutes or until the edges are lightly golden.

9. Cool:

- Allow the koulourakia to cool on the baking sheets for a few minutes before transferring them to a wire rack to cool completely.

10. Enjoy:

- Enjoy these delicious butter cookies with a cup of tea or coffee! Koulourakia are a traditional Greek treat often made during Easter and other festive occasions.

Karidopita (Walnut Cake) Recipe

Ingredients:

For the Cake:

- 1 cup unsalted butter, softened
- 1 cup granulated sugar
- 4 large eggs
- 2 cups all-purpose flour
- 2 teaspoons baking powder
- 1/2 teaspoon baking soda
- 1 teaspoon ground cinnamon
- 1/2 teaspoon ground cloves
- 1/2 teaspoon ground nutmeg
- 1/2 teaspoon salt
- 1 cup Greek yogurt
- 1 cup finely chopped walnuts

For the Syrup:

- 1 cup water
- 1 cup granulated sugar
- 1 cinnamon stick
- 3 whole cloves
- 1 tablespoon honey
- 1 teaspoon lemon juice

Instructions:

1. Preheat Oven:

- Preheat your oven to 350°F (175°C). Grease and flour a 9x13-inch baking pan.

2. Cream Butter and Sugar:

- In a large mixing bowl, cream together the softened butter and sugar until light and fluffy.

3. Add Eggs:

- Add the eggs one at a time, beating well after each addition.

4. Combine Dry Ingredients:

    - In a separate bowl, whisk together the flour, baking powder, baking soda, cinnamon, cloves, nutmeg, and salt.

5. Alternately Add Dry Ingredients and Yogurt:

    - Gradually add the dry ingredients to the butter mixture, alternating with the Greek yogurt. Start and finish with the dry ingredients. Mix until just combined.

6. Add Walnuts:

    - Fold in the finely chopped walnuts into the batter.

7. Bake:

    - Pour the batter into the prepared baking pan and smooth the top. Bake in the preheated oven for about 30-35 minutes or until a toothpick inserted into the center comes out clean.

8. Prepare Syrup:

    - While the cake is baking, prepare the syrup. In a saucepan, combine water, sugar, cinnamon stick, cloves, honey, and lemon juice. Bring to a boil, then reduce heat and simmer for about 10-15 minutes. Remove the cinnamon stick and cloves.

9. Pour Syrup Over Hot Cake:

    - Once the cake is out of the oven and while it's still hot, pour the warm syrup evenly over the top.

10. Cool:

    - Allow the cake to cool completely before serving. The syrup will be absorbed, making the cake moist and flavorful.

11. Slice and Enjoy:

- Slice the Karidopita into squares or diamond shapes. Serve and enjoy this delicious walnut cake with a hint of aromatic spices!

Revani (Semolina Cake) Recipe

Ingredients:

For the Cake:

- 1 cup fine semolina
- 1 cup all-purpose flour
- 1 cup sugar
- 1 cup plain Greek yogurt
- 1 cup unsalted butter, melted
- 4 large eggs
- 1 teaspoon baking powder
- 1/2 teaspoon vanilla extract
- Zest of 1 lemon

For the Syrup:

- 1 cup sugar
- 1 cup water
- Juice of 1 lemon

Instructions:

1. Preheat Oven:

- Preheat your oven to 350°F (175°C). Grease a baking dish (9x13 inches).

2. Prepare the Cake Batter:

- In a large mixing bowl, combine semolina, flour, and baking powder. In a separate bowl, whisk together melted butter and sugar until creamy. Add eggs one at a time, mixing well after each addition. Add Greek yogurt, vanilla extract, and lemon zest. Gradually add the dry ingredients and mix until well combined.

3. Bake:

- Pour the batter into the prepared baking dish and smooth the top. Bake in the preheated oven for about 30-35 minutes or until the top is golden brown and a toothpick inserted into the center comes out clean.

4. Prepare the Syrup:

- While the cake is baking, make the syrup. In a saucepan, combine sugar, water, and lemon juice. Bring to a boil, then reduce heat and simmer for about 10 minutes until the syrup slightly thickens.

5. Soak the Cake:

- Once the cake is out of the oven, immediately pour the warm syrup evenly over the hot cake. Allow the cake to absorb the syrup and cool completely.

6. Serve:

- Cut the Revani into squares or diamonds and serve. Optionally, you can garnish with chopped nuts like pistachios or almonds.

Note:

- Revani is a popular dessert served in many variations across Mediterranean and Middle Eastern regions. Adjust the sweetness and syrup quantities according to your taste preferences.

Diples (Fried Pastry) Recipe

Ingredients:

For the Dough:

- 4 cups all-purpose flour
- 1/2 cup unsalted butter, melted
- 1/2 cup olive oil
- 1/2 cup orange juice
- 1/2 cup white wine
- 1 tablespoon granulated sugar
- 1/2 teaspoon salt

For Frying:

- Vegetable oil for deep frying

For the Syrup:

- 1 cup honey
- 1 cup water
- 1 cup granulated sugar
- Zest of 1 lemon
- Zest of 1 orange
- 1 cinnamon stick

For Garnish:

- Chopped nuts (e.g., walnuts or almonds)
- Ground cinnamon

Instructions:

1. Prepare the Dough:

- In a large mixing bowl, combine the flour, melted butter, olive oil, orange juice, white wine, sugar, and salt. Mix until a soft dough forms. Knead the dough on a floured surface until smooth.

2. Roll and Cut Dough:

- Divide the dough into small portions and roll each piece into thin sheets. Cut the sheets into strips or diamonds, depending on your preference.

3. Heat Oil:

- Heat vegetable oil in a deep fryer or a deep, heavy-bottomed pot to 350°F (175°C).

4. Fry Diples:

- Fry the cut dough pieces in batches until golden brown. Use a slotted spoon to remove them and place them on paper towels to absorb excess oil.

5. Prepare Syrup:

- While the diples are frying, prepare the syrup. In a saucepan, combine honey, water, sugar, lemon zest, orange zest, and a cinnamon stick. Bring to a boil, then reduce heat and simmer for about 10-15 minutes. Remove the cinnamon stick.

6. Coat Diples in Syrup:

- Once the diples are out of the fryer and still hot, dip them into the warm syrup, making sure to coat them evenly. Allow them to soak for a few seconds before removing.

7. Garnish:

- Arrange the coated diples on a serving plate. Sprinkle chopped nuts and ground cinnamon on top.

8. Serve:

- Diples are traditionally served during festive occasions. Enjoy these crispy, honey-soaked pastries with a delightful touch of citrus and cinnamon!

Note: Be cautious when working with hot oil, and make sure to follow safety guidelines for deep frying.

Karydopita (Walnut Cake) Recipe:

Ingredients:

For the Cake:

- 2 cups finely ground walnuts
- 1 cup all-purpose flour
- 1 cup breadcrumbs
- 1 cup sugar
- 1 teaspoon baking powder
- 1/2 teaspoon baking soda
- 1 teaspoon ground cinnamon
- 1/2 teaspoon ground cloves
- 1/2 teaspoon ground nutmeg
- Pinch of salt
- 4 large eggs
- 1 cup Greek yogurt
- 1 cup olive oil
- Zest of 1 orange
- Zest of 1 lemon
- 1 teaspoon vanilla extract

For the Syrup:

- 1 cup water
- 1 cup sugar
- Zest of 1 orange
- Zest of 1 lemon
- 1 cinnamon stick
- 1/2 cup honey

For Serving:

- Your favorite vanilla or walnut ice cream

Instructions:

1. Preheat Oven:

- Preheat your oven to 350°F (175°C). Grease and flour a 9x13-inch baking pan.

2. Prepare the Cake Batter:

    - In a large bowl, combine the ground walnuts, flour, breadcrumbs, sugar, baking powder, baking soda, cinnamon, cloves, nutmeg, and a pinch of salt.

3. Add Wet Ingredients:

    - Add the eggs, Greek yogurt, olive oil, orange zest, lemon zest, and vanilla extract to the dry ingredients. Mix until well combined.

4. Bake:

    - Pour the batter into the prepared baking pan. Bake in the preheated oven for about 40-45 minutes or until a toothpick inserted into the center comes out clean.

5. Prepare the Syrup:

    - While the cake is baking, prepare the syrup. In a saucepan, combine water, sugar, orange zest, lemon zest, cinnamon stick, and honey. Bring to a boil, then reduce heat and simmer for about 10-15 minutes. Remove the cinnamon stick.

6. Soak the Cake:

    - Once the cake is out of the oven and while it's still hot, pour the warm syrup evenly over the top. Allow the cake to absorb the syrup and cool.

7. Serve with Ice Cream:

    - Cut the Karydopita into squares and serve each piece with a scoop of your favorite vanilla or walnut ice cream.

8. Enjoy:

    - Enjoy this delightful Walnut Cake with Ice Cream, combining the rich flavors of the cake with the creamy goodness of the ice cream. It's a wonderful dessert for any occasion!

Sokolatopita (Chocolate Cake) Recipe

Ingredients:

For the Cake:

- 1 cup all-purpose flour
- 1/2 cup cocoa powder
- 1 teaspoon baking powder
- 1/2 teaspoon baking soda
- 1/4 teaspoon salt
- 1/2 cup unsalted butter, softened
- 1 cup granulated sugar
- 3 large eggs
- 1 teaspoon vanilla extract
- 1 cup plain Greek yogurt

For the Chocolate Ganache:

- 1 cup dark chocolate, finely chopped
- 1/2 cup heavy cream
- 2 tablespoons unsalted butter

Optional Toppings:

- Chopped nuts (e.g., walnuts or hazelnuts)
- Powdered sugar for dusting

Instructions:

1. Preheat Oven:

- Preheat your oven to 350°F (175°C). Grease and flour a 9-inch round cake pan.

2. Prepare Dry Ingredients:

- In a bowl, sift together the flour, cocoa powder, baking powder, baking soda, and salt. Set aside.

3. Cream Butter and Sugar:

- In a large mixing bowl, cream together the softened butter and granulated sugar until light and fluffy.

4. Add Eggs and Vanilla:

    - Add the eggs one at a time, beating well after each addition. Mix in the vanilla extract.

5. Add Dry Ingredients Alternately with Yogurt:

    - Gradually add the sifted dry ingredients to the butter mixture, alternating with the Greek yogurt. Begin and end with the dry ingredients. Mix until just combined.

6. Bake:

    - Pour the batter into the prepared cake pan. Smooth the top with a spatula. Bake in the preheated oven for about 25-30 minutes or until a toothpick inserted into the center comes out clean.

7. Prepare Chocolate Ganache:

    - While the cake is baking, prepare the chocolate ganache. In a heatproof bowl, combine the finely chopped dark chocolate, heavy cream, and butter. Melt the mixture over a double boiler or in the microwave, stirring until smooth.

8. Pour Ganache Over Cake:

    - Once the cake is out of the oven and has cooled slightly, pour the chocolate ganache over the top, spreading it evenly.

9. Optional Toppings:

    - Sprinkle chopped nuts over the ganache, and dust with powdered sugar if desired.

10. Cool and Serve:

    - Allow the cake to cool completely before slicing. Serve slices of Sokolatopita and enjoy this rich and decadent chocolate cake!

Note: You can customize this recipe by adding your favorite nuts or even a scoop of ice cream on the side for an extra treat.

Greek-Style Fougasse Recipe:

Ingredients:

For the Dough:

- 4 cups all-purpose flour
- 1 packet (2 1/4 teaspoons) active dry yeast
- 1 1/2 cups warm water
- 1 teaspoon sugar
- 1 teaspoon salt
- 1/4 cup olive oil

For the Filling:

- 1 cup feta cheese, crumbled
- 1/2 cup Kalamata olives, pitted and chopped
- 1/4 cup fresh oregano, chopped
- 1/4 cup sun-dried tomatoes, chopped

For Topping:

- Olive oil for brushing
- Coarse sea salt
- Freshly ground black pepper

Instructions:

1. Activate Yeast:

- In a bowl, combine warm water, sugar, and yeast. Let it sit for about 5-10 minutes until it becomes frothy.

2. Prepare Dough:

- In a large mixing bowl, combine the flour and salt. Make a well in the center and pour in the activated yeast mixture and olive oil. Mix until a dough forms.

3. Knead:

- Turn the dough onto a floured surface and knead for about 8-10 minutes until it becomes smooth and elastic.

4. First Rise:

    - Place the dough in a lightly oiled bowl, cover it with a kitchen towel, and let it rise in a warm place for about 1-2 hours or until it doubles in size.

5. Preheat Oven:

    - Preheat your oven to 400°F (200°C).

6. Shape Dough:

    - Punch down the risen dough and turn it onto a floured surface. Roll it into a large oval or rectangle.

7. Add Filling:

    - Sprinkle the crumbled feta, chopped olives, oregano, and sun-dried tomatoes evenly over the rolled-out dough.

8. Shape Fougasse:

    - Using a sharp knife, make several slashes or cuts in the dough to resemble leaf veins or an ear of wheat. Gently pull apart the cuts to create openings.

9. Second Rise:

    - Place the shaped dough on a baking sheet lined with parchment paper. Cover it with a kitchen towel and let it rise for another 15-20 minutes.

10. Bake:

    - Brush the Fougasse with olive oil and sprinkle with coarse sea salt and freshly ground black pepper. Bake in the preheated oven for about 20-25 minutes or until golden brown.

11. Cool:

- Allow the Greek-style Fougasse to cool slightly before slicing. Serve and enjoy this flavorful bread with a touch of Mediterranean flair!

This Greek-inspired Fougasse is perfect for sharing and pairs well with a variety of dips, spreads, or enjoyed on its own.

Tiropita (Greek Cheese Pie) Recipe

Ingredients:

For the Filling:

- 2 cups feta cheese, crumbled
- 1 cup ricotta cheese
- 1 cup Greek yogurt
- 2 large eggs
- 1 cup fresh parsley, chopped
- Salt and pepper to taste

For the Dough:

- 1 package (about 1 pound) phyllo dough, thawed
- 1 cup unsalted butter, melted

For Brushing Between Layers:

- Olive oil or melted butter

Instructions:

1. Preheat Oven:

- Preheat your oven to 350°F (175°C). Grease a baking dish (9x13 inches).

2. Prepare Filling:

- In a large mixing bowl, combine the crumbled feta, ricotta cheese, Greek yogurt, eggs, chopped parsley, salt, and pepper. Mix well until all ingredients are evenly incorporated.

3. Layer Phyllo Dough:

- Lay one sheet of phyllo dough in the greased baking dish, allowing the edges to hang over the sides. Brush the sheet lightly with olive oil or melted butter. Repeat with several more sheets, brushing each layer.

4. Add Cheese Filling:

- Spread a portion of the cheese filling evenly over the layered phyllo dough.

5. Repeat Layers:

- Continue layering phyllo sheets and cheese filling until all the filling is used, finishing with a top layer of phyllo sheets. Remember to brush each layer with olive oil or melted butter.

6. Fold Edges:

- Fold the overhanging edges of the phyllo dough back over the top to create a neat border.

7. Score the Top:

- Using a sharp knife, score the top layers of the phyllo into squares or diamond shapes. This will make it easier to slice once baked.

8. Bake:

- Bake in the preheated oven for about 45-50 minutes or until the tiropita is golden brown and crispy.

9. Cool and Slice:

- Allow the tiropita to cool slightly before slicing along the scored lines.

10. Serve:

- Serve the tiropita warm or at room temperature. It's a delightful appetizer or main dish, perfect for any occasion.

Note: Tiropita can be enjoyed on its own or served with a side of Greek salad for a complete meal. Adjust the filling ingredients according to your taste preferences.

Bougatsa (Custard-Filled Pastry) Recipe

Ingredients:

For the Custard Filling:

- 2 cups whole milk
- 1 cup semolina flour
- 1 cup granulated sugar
- 1 teaspoon vanilla extract
- 2 large eggs

For the Pastry:

- 1 package (about 1 pound) phyllo dough, thawed
- 1 cup unsalted butter, melted
- Powdered sugar for dusting

Instructions:

1. Preheat Oven:

- Preheat your oven to 350°F (175°C). Grease a baking dish (9x13 inches).

2. Prepare Custard Filling:

- In a saucepan, heat the milk over medium heat until it's warm but not boiling. In a bowl, whisk together the semolina flour, sugar, vanilla extract, and eggs. Gradually add the warm milk to the mixture while whisking continuously.

3. Cook Custard:

- Pour the custard mixture back into the saucepan and cook over medium heat, stirring constantly, until the mixture thickens. Remove from heat and let it cool.

4. Layer Phyllo Dough:

- Lay one sheet of phyllo dough in the greased baking dish, allowing the edges to hang over the sides. Brush the sheet lightly with melted butter. Repeat with several more sheets, brushing each layer.

5. Add Custard Filling:

- Spread a layer of the cooled custard over the layered phyllo dough.

6. Repeat Layers:

- Continue layering phyllo sheets and custard filling until all the custard is used, finishing with a top layer of phyllo sheets. Remember to brush each layer with melted butter.

7. Fold Edges:

- Fold the overhanging edges of the phyllo dough back over the top to create a neat border.

8. Bake:

- Bake in the preheated oven for about 45-50 minutes or until the bougatsa is golden brown and crispy.

9. Cool and Dust with Powdered Sugar:

- Allow the bougatsa to cool slightly before dusting with powdered sugar.

10. Serve:

- Serve the bougatsa warm, cut into squares. Enjoy this delightful custard-filled pastry, a popular Greek treat!

Note: Bougatsa can be made with various fillings, including custard, cheese, or minced meat. Adjust the filling according to your preferences.

Koulouri Thessalonikis (Sesame Seed Bread Rings) Recipe

Ingredients:

For the Dough:

- 4 cups all-purpose flour
- 1 tablespoon active dry yeast
- 1 teaspoon sugar
- 1 1/2 cups warm water
- 1/4 cup olive oil
- 1 teaspoon salt

For Coating:

- 1 cup sesame seeds
- 1/2 cup water

Instructions:

1. Activate Yeast:

- In a small bowl, combine warm water, sugar, and yeast. Let it sit for about 5-10 minutes until it becomes frothy.

2. Prepare Dough:

- In a large mixing bowl, combine the flour and salt. Make a well in the center and pour in the activated yeast mixture and olive oil. Mix until a dough forms.

3. Knead:

- Turn the dough onto a floured surface and knead for about 8-10 minutes until it becomes smooth and elastic.

4. First Rise:

- Place the dough in a lightly oiled bowl, cover it with a kitchen towel, and let it rise in a warm place for about 1-2 hours or until it doubles in size.

5. Preheat Oven:

- Preheat your oven to 375°F (190°C). Line baking sheets with parchment paper.

6. Shape Koulouri:

- Punch down the risen dough and divide it into small portions. Roll each portion into a long rope, and then shape the ropes into rings. Place the rings on the prepared baking sheets.

7. Coating:

- In a shallow dish, combine sesame seeds and water. Dip each ring into the sesame seed mixture, ensuring it's well-coated on all sides.

8. Second Rise:

- Allow the coated koulouri to rise for an additional 15-20 minutes.

9. Bake:

- Bake in the preheated oven for about 20-25 minutes or until the koulouri is golden brown and sounds hollow when tapped on the bottom.

10. Cool:

- Allow the koulouri to cool on a wire rack.

11. Serve:

- Serve these delightful sesame seed bread rings with your favorite spreads, cheeses, or enjoy them on their own. They are perfect for breakfast or as a snack!

Note: Koulouri Thessalonikis is a popular street food in Thessaloniki, Greece. It's a versatile bread ring that can be enjoyed in various ways.

Lagana (Clean Monday Flatbread) Recipe

Ingredients:

For the Dough:

- 4 cups all-purpose flour
- 1 packet (about 2 1/4 teaspoons) active dry yeast
- 1 teaspoon sugar
- 1 1/2 cups warm water
- 2 tablespoons olive oil
- 1 teaspoon salt

For Topping:

- Sesame seeds
- Olive oil for brushing

Instructions:

1. Activate Yeast:

- In a small bowl, combine warm water, sugar, and yeast. Let it sit for about 5-10 minutes until it becomes frothy.

2. Prepare Dough:

- In a large mixing bowl, combine the flour and salt. Make a well in the center and pour in the activated yeast mixture and olive oil. Mix until a dough forms.

3. Knead:

- Turn the dough onto a floured surface and knead for about 8-10 minutes until it becomes smooth and elastic.

4. First Rise:

- Place the dough in a lightly oiled bowl, cover it with a kitchen towel, and let it rise in a warm place for about 1-2 hours or until it doubles in size.

5. Preheat Oven:

- Preheat your oven to 400°F (200°C).

6. Shape Lagana:

- Punch down the risen dough and divide it into two portions. Roll out each portion into a rectangular shape on a floured surface.

7. Topping:

- Place the rolled-out dough on baking sheets lined with parchment paper. Brush the top with olive oil and sprinkle sesame seeds generously.

8. Second Rise:

- Allow the lagana to rise for an additional 15-20 minutes.

9. Bake:

- Bake in the preheated oven for about 20-25 minutes or until the lagana is golden brown and sounds hollow when tapped on the bottom.

10. Cool:

- Allow the lagana to cool on a wire rack.

11. Serve:

- Serve the lagana as a traditional dish for Clean Monday or enjoy it as a delicious flatbread throughout the year. It pairs well with olives, cheese, and other Mediterranean delights.

Note: Clean Monday, also known as "Kathara Deftera" in Greek, marks the beginning of Lent in the Eastern Orthodox Christian tradition, and lagana is a special bread prepared for this occasion.

Greek Frappe Coffee Recipe

Ingredients:

- 2 teaspoons instant coffee (Greek coffee, if available)
- 2 teaspoons sugar (adjust to taste)
- Cold water
- Ice cubes
- Milk (optional)
- Evaporated milk or condensed milk (optional)
- Mint leaves for garnish (optional)

Instructions:

1. Prepare Instant Coffee:

- In a shaker or blender, combine instant coffee and sugar. Adjust the sugar amount according to your preference for sweetness.

2. Add Water:

- Add a small amount of cold water to the shaker. The traditional Greek frappe has three levels of sweetness: "sketos" (unsweetened), "metrios" (medium sweet), and "glykos" (sweet). Adjust sugar accordingly.

3. Shake or Blend:

- Shake the mixture vigorously in a shaker or blend using a blender until it becomes frothy and forms a thick foam on top.

4. Prepare Glass:

- Fill a glass with ice cubes. If you prefer a stronger coffee flavor, you can use coffee ice cubes.

5. Pour the Coffee:

- Pour the frothy coffee mixture over the ice cubes.

6. Add Milk (Optional):

- If desired, add a splash of regular milk, evaporated milk, or condensed milk for creaminess. Adjust the amount to your liking.

7. Garnish (Optional):

- Garnish with mint leaves for a refreshing touch.

8. Stir and Enjoy:

- Stir the frappe well to combine the coffee with the ice and milk. Enjoy your Greek frappe coffee!

Tips:

- Use a tall glass to allow room for the frothy coffee.
- Experiment with the sugar and milk amounts to find your preferred level of sweetness and creaminess.
- Serve with a straw for easy sipping.

Greek frappe coffee is a popular and refreshing beverage, especially during the warm summer months. It's a delightful way to enjoy coffee with a frothy and chilled twist.

Greek Mountain Tea (Tsai Tou Vounou) Recipe

Ingredients:

- 1 tablespoon dried Greek mountain tea (Tsai Tou Vounou)
- 2 cups water
- Honey or lemon (optional, for serving)

Instructions:

1. Boil Water:

- Bring 2 cups of water to a boil in a pot.

2. Add Mountain Tea:

- Once the water is boiling, add the dried Greek mountain tea to the pot.

3. Simmer:

- Reduce the heat to low and let the tea simmer for about 5-10 minutes. This allows the flavors of the mountain tea to infuse into the water.

4. Strain:

- After simmering, strain the tea to remove the tea leaves. You can use a fine mesh strainer or a tea infuser.

5. Serve:

- Pour the strained tea into cups.

6. Optional Additions:

- If desired, you can add honey or a squeeze of lemon to taste. Greek mountain tea is often enjoyed with honey for sweetness.

7. Enjoy:

- Sip and enjoy your Greek mountain tea. It has a mild and slightly earthy flavor, making it a soothing and aromatic herbal tea.

Note:

- Greek mountain tea is known for its potential health benefits and is often consumed for its calming properties.
- Feel free to adjust the quantity of mountain tea and steeping time based on your taste preferences.
- This herbal tea is commonly consumed in Greece and other Mediterranean countries, especially during the colder months or when someone is feeling under the weather.

Tiropita (Cheese Pie) Recipe

Ingredients:

For the Filling:

- 2 cups feta cheese, crumbled
- 1 cup ricotta cheese
- 1 cup Greek yogurt
- 2 large eggs
- 1 cup fresh parsley, chopped
- Salt and pepper to taste

For the Dough:

- 1 package (about 1 pound) phyllo dough, thawed
- 1 cup unsalted butter, melted

Instructions:

1. Preheat Oven:

- Preheat your oven to 350°F (175°C). Grease a baking dish (9x13 inches).

2. Prepare Filling:

- In a large mixing bowl, combine the crumbled feta, ricotta cheese, Greek yogurt, eggs, chopped parsley, salt, and pepper. Mix well until all ingredients are evenly incorporated.

3. Layer Phyllo Dough:

- Lay one sheet of phyllo dough in the greased baking dish, allowing the edges to hang over the sides. Brush the sheet lightly with melted butter. Repeat with several more sheets, brushing each layer.

4. Add Cheese Filling:

- Spread a portion of the cheese filling evenly over the layered phyllo dough.

5. Repeat Layers:

   - Continue layering phyllo sheets and cheese filling until all the filling is used, finishing with a top layer of phyllo sheets. Remember to brush each layer with melted butter.

6. Fold Edges:

   - Fold the overhanging edges of the phyllo dough back over the top to create a neat border.

7. Score the Top:

   - Using a sharp knife, score the top layers of the phyllo into squares or diamond shapes. This will make it easier to slice once baked.

8. Bake:

   - Bake in the preheated oven for about 45-50 minutes or until the tiropita is golden brown and crispy.

9. Cool and Slice:

   - Allow the tiropita to cool slightly before slicing along the scored lines.

10. Serve:

    - Serve the tiropita warm or at room temperature. It's a delightful appetizer or main dish, perfect for any occasion.

Note: Tiropita can be enjoyed on its own or served with a side of Greek salad for a complete meal. Adjust the filling ingredients according to your taste preferences.

Ouzo Cocktail Recipe

Ingredients:

- 2 oz ouzo
- 1 oz simple syrup
- 3/4 oz fresh lemon juice
- Ice cubes
- Lemon twist or slice, for garnish
- Optional: Splash of club soda

Instructions:

1. Prepare Simple Syrup:

    - In a small saucepan, combine equal parts water and sugar. Heat over medium heat, stirring until the sugar dissolves. Allow it to cool before using.

2. Chill Glass:

    - Place your serving glass in the freezer for a few minutes to chill.

3. Shake Ingredients:

    - Fill a cocktail shaker with ice cubes. Add ouzo, simple syrup, and fresh lemon juice to the shaker.

4. Shake Well:

    - Shake the ingredients vigorously for about 15-20 seconds to chill the mixture.

5. Strain into Glass:

    - Strain the cocktail into the chilled glass. You can use a fine mesh strainer to catch any ice chips.

6. Optional: Add Club Soda:

    - For a slightly effervescent touch, add a splash of club soda to the cocktail and give it a gentle stir.

7. Garnish:

- Garnish the cocktail with a lemon twist or slice for a citrusy aroma.

8. Enjoy:

- Sip and enjoy your Ouzo Cocktail. The anise flavor of ouzo combined with the sweetness of the syrup and the tartness of lemon creates a harmonious and refreshing drink.

Note:

- Adjust the sweetness by adding more or less simple syrup according to your taste preferences.
- Some variations of this cocktail may include muddled fresh mint or a few drops of bitters for added complexity.
- Ouzo is a strong spirit, so sip responsibly. Cheers!

Homemade Mastiha Liqueur Recipe

Ingredients:

- 1 cup mastiha liqueur crystals or mastiha liqueur extract (available at specialty stores or online)
- 1 bottle (750 ml) vodka or neutral grain spirit
- 1 cup simple syrup (equal parts water and sugar, dissolved)

Instructions:

1. Prepare Mastiha Liqueur Base:

   - If you have mastiha liqueur crystals, crush them to a powder using a mortar and pestle. If you have mastiha liqueur extract, use it directly.

2. Combine Ingredients:

   - In a large, sealable glass jar or bottle, combine the mastiha liqueur crystals or extract with the vodka.

3. Seal and Infuse:

   - Seal the jar or bottle tightly and place it in a cool, dark place. Let the mixture infuse for at least 1 to 2 weeks. You can shake the bottle occasionally to help with the infusion process.

4. Strain:

   - After the infusion period, strain the mixture to remove any solid particles. You can use a fine mesh strainer or cheesecloth for this.

5. Prepare Simple Syrup:

   - In a saucepan, combine equal parts water and sugar. Heat over medium heat, stirring until the sugar completely dissolves. Allow the simple syrup to cool.

6. Add Simple Syrup:

- Mix the simple syrup with the strained mastiha-infused vodka. Adjust the sweetness to your liking by adding more or less simple syrup.

7. Bottle:

- Transfer the Mastiha Liqueur to a clean, sealable bottle for storage.

8. Aging (Optional):

- For additional flavor development, let the Mastiha Liqueur age for another 1 to 2 weeks in the bottle.

9. Serve:

- Serve the Mastiha Liqueur chilled or over ice. It can also be used in various cocktails or enjoyed as an aperitif.

Note:

- Mastiha Liqueur has a distinct piney, resinous flavor with a hint of sweetness. The flavor can be intense, so it's often served in small quantities.
- This homemade version allows you to adjust the sweetness and overall flavor profile according to your preferences. Experiment with ratios to find the perfect balance for your taste.
- Enjoy responsibly!

How Retsina Wine is Made:

Ingredients:

- White wine grapes (typically Assyrtiko, Roditis, or Savatiano)
- Pine resin
- Water
- Optionally, sulfur dioxide (used as a preservative)

Process:

1. Grape Harvest:

- The winemaking process begins with the harvest of white wine grapes. The most common grape varieties used for Retsina include Assyrtiko, Roditis, and Savatiano.

2. Crushing and Pressing:

- The harvested grapes are crushed, and the juice is extracted. The grape juice is then pressed to separate the liquid from the solids.

3. Fermentation:

- The grape juice undergoes fermentation, where yeast converts the sugars in the juice into alcohol. This is a crucial step in winemaking.

4. Addition of Pine Resin:

- Pine resin is added to the fermenting grape juice. The amount of resin added can vary depending on the desired flavor profile. The resin is typically obtained from Aleppo pine trees.

5. Aging:

- The wine, now infused with the pine resin, is allowed to age. This can take place in stainless steel tanks, amphorae, or traditional wooden barrels. The aging process allows the flavors to meld and the characteristic taste of Retsina to develop.

6. Filtration and Clarification:

- After aging, the wine is filtered and clarified to remove any sediment or impurities.

7. Bottling:

- The clarified Retsina wine is bottled, often in amber-colored bottles to protect it from light, which can alter its flavor.

8. Maturation (Optional):

- Some producers choose to allow the bottled Retsina to mature further, developing additional complexity and character.

9. Enjoying Retsina:

- Retsina is typically served chilled and is a popular accompaniment to Greek cuisine. Its unique taste, with notes of resin and pine, makes it a distinctive and traditional Greek wine.

Note:

- Retsina's flavor can be an acquired taste for those unfamiliar with it. It pairs well with various Greek dishes, especially seafood and mezze (appetizers).
- The addition of pine resin was historically used as a preservative, helping to protect the wine during long journeys and storage.
- Retsina comes in different styles, from dry to semi-sweet, so the flavor can vary among different producers.

Bougatsa me Krema (Custard-Filled Pastry) Recipe

Ingredients:

For the Custard Filling:

- 2 cups whole milk
- 1 cup granulated sugar
- 1/2 cup semolina flour
- 4 large eggs
- 1 teaspoon vanilla extract
- 1/4 cup unsalted butter

For the Phyllo Dough:

- 1 package (about 1 pound) phyllo dough, thawed
- 1 cup unsalted butter, melted
- Powdered sugar for dusting

Instructions:

1. Prepare Custard Filling:

- In a saucepan, heat the milk over medium heat until it's warm but not boiling. In a bowl, whisk together sugar, semolina flour, eggs, and vanilla extract.

2. Cook Custard:

- Slowly pour the egg mixture into the warm milk, whisking constantly to prevent lumps. Add the unsalted butter and continue to cook over medium heat, stirring continuously until the mixture thickens into a custard. Remove from heat and let it cool.

3. Preheat Oven:

- Preheat your oven to 350°F (175°C). Grease a baking dish (9x13 inches).

4. Assemble the Bougatsa:

- Lay one sheet of phyllo dough in the greased baking dish, allowing the edges to hang over the sides. Brush the sheet lightly with melted butter. Repeat with several more sheets, brushing each layer.

5. Add Custard Filling:

- Spread a layer of the cooled custard over the layered phyllo dough.

6. Repeat Layers:

- Continue layering phyllo sheets and custard filling until all the custard is used, finishing with a top layer of phyllo sheets. Remember to brush each layer with melted butter.

7. Fold Edges:

- Fold the overhanging edges of the phyllo dough back over the top to create a neat border.

8. Score the Top:

- Using a sharp knife, score the top layers of the phyllo into squares or diamond shapes. This will make it easier to slice once baked.

9. Bake:

- Bake in the preheated oven for about 45-50 minutes or until the bougatsa is golden brown and crispy.

10. Cool and Dust with Powdered Sugar:

- Allow the bougatsa to cool slightly before dusting with powdered sugar.

11. Serve:

- Serve the bougatsa warm, cut into squares. Enjoy this delightful custard-filled pastry, a popular Greek treat!

Note: Bougatsa me Krema is often enjoyed as a breakfast pastry or dessert. Adjust the sweetness by adding more or less sugar to the custard filling according to your taste preferences.

Strapatsada (Tomato and Scrambled Eggs) Recipe

Ingredients:

- 4 large tomatoes, ripe and diced
- 1 onion, finely chopped
- 4-6 eggs
- 1/4 cup extra virgin olive oil
- Salt and pepper, to taste
- Fresh parsley, chopped (for garnish)
- Feta cheese (optional, for serving)

Instructions:

1. Prepare Ingredients:

- Dice the tomatoes and finely chop the onion.

2. Sauté Onions:

- In a large skillet, heat the olive oil over medium heat. Add the chopped onion and sauté until softened and translucent.

3. Add Tomatoes:

- Add the diced tomatoes to the skillet. Season with salt and pepper to taste. Cook the tomatoes until they release their juices and become soft.

4. Scramble Eggs:

- Push the tomato mixture to the sides of the skillet, creating a well in the center. Crack the eggs into the well and scramble them using a spatula.

5. Combine Ingredients:

- As the eggs start to set, mix them with the tomato mixture. Continue cooking and stirring until the eggs are fully cooked.

6. Adjust Seasoning:

- Taste and adjust the seasoning with more salt and pepper if needed.

7. Garnish:

    - Sprinkle fresh chopped parsley over the strapatsada for a burst of freshness.

8. Serve:

    - Serve the strapatsada hot, straight from the skillet. Optionally, crumble feta cheese over the top for added creaminess and flavor.

9. Enjoy:

    - Enjoy strapatsada as a delicious and hearty breakfast or brunch dish. Serve it with crusty bread or pita for a complete meal.

Note:

- Strapatsada is a versatile dish, and you can customize it by adding ingredients like bell peppers, garlic, or even a touch of chili flakes for some heat.
- The dish is commonly enjoyed in Mediterranean cuisine and is perfect for using ripe, seasonal tomatoes.

Koulouri Thessalonikis (Sesame Seed Bread Rings) Recipe

Ingredients:

For the Dough:

- 4 cups all-purpose flour
- 1 tablespoon active dry yeast
- 1 teaspoon sugar
- 1 1/2 cups warm water
- 2 tablespoons olive oil
- 1 teaspoon salt

For Coating:

- 1 cup sesame seeds
- 1/2 cup water

Instructions:

1. Activate Yeast:

- In a small bowl, combine warm water, sugar, and yeast. Let it sit for about 5-10 minutes until it becomes frothy.

2. Prepare Dough:

- In a large mixing bowl, combine the flour and salt. Make a well in the center and pour in the activated yeast mixture and olive oil. Mix until a dough forms.

3. Knead:

- Turn the dough onto a floured surface and knead for about 8-10 minutes until it becomes smooth and elastic.

4. First Rise:

- Place the dough in a lightly oiled bowl, cover it with a kitchen towel, and let it rise in a warm place for about 1-2 hours or until it doubles in size.

5. Preheat Oven:

   - Preheat your oven to 375°F (190°C). Line baking sheets with parchment paper.

6. Shape Koulouri:

   - Punch down the risen dough and divide it into small portions. Roll each portion into a long rope, and then shape the ropes into rings. Place the rings on the prepared baking sheets.

7. Coating:

   - In a shallow dish, combine sesame seeds and water. Dip each ring into the sesame seed mixture, ensuring it's well-coated on all sides.

8. Second Rise:

   - Allow the coated koulouri to rise for an additional 15-20 minutes.

9. Bake:

   - Bake in the preheated oven for about 20-25 minutes or until the koulouri is golden brown and sounds hollow when tapped on the bottom.

10. Cool:

    - Allow the koulouri to cool on a wire rack.

11. Serve:

    - Serve these delightful sesame seed bread rings with your favorite spreads, cheeses, or enjoy them on their own. They are perfect for breakfast or as a snack!

Note: Koulouri Thessalonikis is a popular street food in Thessaloniki, Greece. It's a versatile bread ring that can be enjoyed in various ways. Adjust the size of the rings and sesame coating according to your preference.

Greek Yogurt with Honey and Nuts Recipe

Ingredients:

- 1 cup Greek yogurt
- 2 tablespoons honey (adjust to taste)
- 1/4 cup mixed nuts (such as walnuts, almonds, or pistachios), chopped
- Fresh mint leaves for garnish (optional)

Instructions:

1. Prepare the Greek Yogurt:

   - Spoon the Greek yogurt into a serving bowl or individual bowls.

2. Drizzle with Honey:

   - Drizzle honey over the Greek yogurt. Adjust the amount of honey based on your desired level of sweetness.

3. Add Chopped Nuts:

   - Sprinkle the chopped nuts over the yogurt and honey. You can use a mix of your favorite nuts for variety and added texture.

4. Optional Garnish:

   - If desired, garnish with fresh mint leaves for a touch of freshness.

5. Serve and Enjoy:

   - Serve the Greek yogurt with honey and nuts immediately. Use a spoon to mix the ingredients together before each bite to ensure a delightful combination of creamy yogurt, sweet honey, and crunchy nuts.

Variations:

- Fruit Additions: Enhance the dish by adding fresh fruits such as berries, sliced bananas, or diced peaches.

- Cinnamon Twist: Sprinkle a pinch of ground cinnamon over the yogurt for a warm and aromatic flavor.
- Chia Seeds: For added nutrition and texture, sprinkle chia seeds on top of the Greek yogurt.
- Vanilla Extract: Add a drop of vanilla extract to the honey for a subtle vanilla flavor.

Note:

- This Greek Yogurt with Honey and Nuts recipe is not only delicious but also a nutritious and satisfying snack or breakfast option.
- Experiment with different combinations of nuts and fruits to create your own personalized version of this classic Greek treat.

Tyropita (Cheese Pie) Recipe

Ingredients:

For the Filling:

- 3 cups feta cheese, crumbled
- 1 cup ricotta cheese
- 1 cup Greek yogurt
- 3 large eggs
- 1/4 cup fresh parsley, chopped
- Salt and pepper, to taste

For the Phyllo Dough:

- 1 package (about 1 pound) phyllo dough, thawed
- 1 cup unsalted butter, melted

Instructions:

1. Preheat Oven:

- Preheat your oven to 350°F (175°C). Grease a baking dish (9x13 inches).

2. Prepare Filling:

- In a large mixing bowl, combine crumbled feta, ricotta cheese, Greek yogurt, eggs, chopped parsley, salt, and pepper. Mix well until all ingredients are evenly incorporated.

3. Layer Phyllo Dough:

- Lay one sheet of phyllo dough in the greased baking dish, allowing the edges to hang over the sides. Brush the sheet lightly with melted butter. Repeat with several more sheets, brushing each layer.

4. Add Cheese Filling:

- Spread a portion of the cheese filling evenly over the layered phyllo dough.

5. Repeat Layers:

- Continue layering phyllo sheets and cheese filling until all the filling is used, finishing with a top layer of phyllo sheets. Remember to brush each layer with melted butter.

6. Fold Edges:

- Fold the overhanging edges of the phyllo dough back over the top to create a neat border.

7. Score the Top:

- Using a sharp knife, score the top layers of the phyllo into squares or diamond shapes. This will make it easier to slice once baked.

8. Bake:

- Bake in the preheated oven for about 45-50 minutes or until the tyropita is golden brown and crispy.

9. Cool and Slice:

- Allow the tyropita to cool slightly before slicing along the scored lines.

10. Serve:

- Serve the tyropita warm or at room temperature. It can be enjoyed as an appetizer, snack, or part of a meal.

Note:

- Tyropita is a versatile dish, and you can customize it by adding herbs, spinach, or other ingredients to the cheese filling.
- Adjust the quantity of phyllo sheets and baking time based on your desired level of crispiness.

www.ingramcontent.com/pod-product-compliance
Lightning Source LLC
LaVergne TN
LVHW081553060526
838201LV00054B/1881